Everyday BIBLE TRIVIA COLLECTION

365 QUIZZES!

Everyday BIBLE

TRIVIA COLLECTION

365 QUIZZES!

BARBOUR
PUBLISHING

ISBN 978-1-63609-426-7

Published by Barbour Publishing, Inc., 1810 Barbour Drive, Uhrichsville, Ohio 44683, www.barbourbooks.com

Our mission is to inspire the world with the life-changing message of the Bible.

ecpa Member of the Evangelical Christian Publishers Association

Printed in the United States of America.

Introduction

What was Matthew's occupation before he became a disciple of Jesus?

What kind of animal helped Samson burn the grain fields of his enemies?

a) lightning bugs
b) lions
c) donkeys
d) foxes

True or False: Another name for Jesus' mother is Mary Magdalene.

Complete the scripture:

Do not let the _____ _____ _____ while you are still angry (Ephesians 4:26 NIV).

Match: Vashti. . .

a) another name for Esther
b) queen of Persia
c) Mordecai's cousin

Test your scriptural knowledge with the *Everyday Bible Trivia Collection*! Each day for an entire year, you'll find five questions covering the fascinating people and places, times and teachings, objects and oddities of the Bible. Can you answer them correctly?

Inside this book, you'll be tested by multiple-choice questions, fill-in-the-blanks, open-ended queries, true or false statements, matching quizzes, and "Connect the Thoughts" stumpers. To Connect the Thoughts, you'll need to determine the common theme among three seemingly unrelated ideas. For example, the connection among

- a worm-eaten plant
- an unusual fish
- a sinful city of 120,000

would be *the story of Jonah*. Answers for each day's questions are located at the bottom of each page—upside down, so you can't peek.

Ready to begin? Good. . .because you'll be testing your Bible knowledge every day for the next twelve months. The *Everyday Bible Trivia Collection* promises a whole year of fun!

Day 1

1. What sound, according to the apostle Paul, causes every knee in heaven to bow?

2. What, in addition to *grace*, did the apostle John say Jesus, the Word, was "full of"?
   a) truth
   b) power
   c) love
   d) hope

3. True or False: Although Jesus was rejected in many cities, He was warmly received in His hometown of Nazareth.

4. What did Jesus do to serve His disciples at the Last Supper?

5. Connect the Thoughts:
   Egypt
   Capernaum
   Nazareth

ANSWERS

1. the name of Jesus (Philippians 2:10 NIV)
2. a (John 1:14 KJV)
3. False (Matthew 13:57)
4. He washed their feet (John 13:14)
5. places Jesus lived (Matthew 2:13–15; Matthew 4:12–13; Luke 4:14–16)

Day 2

1. King Artaxerxes ordered that
    a) a festival be held each year to honor Jerusalem.
    b) everyone in Persia was to worship Jehovah.
    c) Jerusalem not be rebuilt until his command.
    d) no Jew was to work more than eight hours a day.

2. Which son of Jesse would succeed Saul as king?

3. Match: Vashti. . .
    a) another name for Esther
    b) queen of Persia
    c) Mordecai's cousin

4. Jonah told the Ninevites that they had how many days left before God would destroy them?

5. What Old Testament prophet was a shepherd from Tekoa?
    a) Micah
    b) Nahum
    c) Amos
    d) Zechariah

ANSWERS

1. c (Ezra 4:12, 21)
2. David (1 Samuel 16:1, 11–13)
3. b (Esther 1:2–3, 9)
4. forty (Jonah 3:4)
5. c (Amos 1:1)

Day 3

1. What problem was the brave army commander Naaman healed of?
   a) blindness
   b) leprosy
   c) fever
   d) a hunched back

2. At what site did the Lord confound the language of the earth?

3. What angel announced the birth of Jesus to His mother, Mary?

4. Job's children were killed by
   a) Assyrians.
   b) fire.
   c) wind.
   d) hail.

5. What sea, according to the book of Hebrews, was crossed by the Israelites, by faith, "as by dry land"?

ANSWERS

1. b (2 Kings 5:1, 14)
2. Babel (Genesis 11:9)
3. Gabriel (Luke 1:26–31)
4. c (Job 1:1, 18–19)
5. the Red Sea (Hebrews 11:29 KJV)

Day 4

1. When a Christian is too sad or upset to pray, what does the Holy Spirit do?

2. Complete the scripture:
   And as soon as we had heard these things, our hearts did melt, neither did there remain any more courage in any man, because of you: for the LORD your ____, he is ____ in heaven above, and in earth beneath.

3. According to the Lord's Prayer, where is God the Father?

4. Connect the Thoughts:
   immortal
   invisible
   the only wise

5. The disciples received the Holy Spirit during what special holiday?
   a) the Day of Atonement
   b) Pentecost
   c) Passover
   d) the Feast of Purim

ANSWERS

1. The Holy Spirit tells God what the Christian needs (Romans 8:26).
2. God, God (Joshua 2:11 KJV)
3. in heaven (Luke 11:2)
4. God (1 Timothy 1:17 KJV)
5. b (Acts 2:1–4)

Day 5

1. How many letters did Paul write to the Corinthians?

2. Match: Aquila and Priscilla. . .
   a) sold idols in Ephesus.
   b) dealt in fine linen and wool.
   c) were tentmakers.

3. What were the Bereans famous for?

4. True or False: Eutychus was an old woman.

5. Complete the scripture:
   For she said within herself, If I may but ____ his garment, I shall be whole.

ANSWERS

1. two
2. c (Acts 18:2–3)
3. searching the scriptures (Acts 17:10–11)
4. False (Acts 20:9)
5. touch (Matthew 9:21 KJV)

Day 6

1. Bethlehem is the city of ____.

2. The name of the place where the Thessalonians lived was
   a) Thesis.
   b) Thessalonica.
   c) Toronto.
   d) Thessa.

3. What river stopped flowing when priests carrying the ark reached the water's edge?

4. Connect the Thoughts:
   the Philippian jail
   Jesus' tomb
   Mt. Sinai

5. Match: Valley of Kidron. . .
   a) where Jesus gave the Beatitudes
   b) where Jesus brought Lazarus back from the dead
   c) near where Jesus was arrested

ANSWERS

1. David (Luke 2:4)
2. b
3. Jordan (Joshua 3:15–16)
4. sites of earthquakes (Acts 16:12–26; Matthew 28:1–6; Exodus 19:18)
5. c (John 18:1, 12 NIV)

Day 7

1. What are two of the four ways Luke says the young boy Jesus grew up?

2. What problem did Jesus heal two men of, saying, "According to your faith be it unto you"?
   a) leprosy
   b) blindness
   c) demon possession
   d) lameness

3. Connect the Thoughts:
   turn stones into bread
   jump from the top of the temple
   worship the devil

4. Jesus taught in stories. What are they called?

5. Complete the scripture:
   Come unto me, all ye that labour and are heavy laden,
   and I will give you ____.

ANSWERS

1. in wisdom, stature, favor with God, and favor with men (Luke 2:52)
2. b (Matthew 9:27–30 KJV)
3. the temptation of Christ (Matthew 4:1–11)
4. parables
5. rest (Matthew 11:28 KJV)

Day 8

1. David was skillful at playing the
    a) electric organ.
    b) kazoo.
    c) accordion.
    d) harp.

2. What precious metal covered the ark and its carrying poles?

3. Connect the Thoughts:
    a mount
    groves
    Noah's dove

4. Match: Pillar of fire. . .
    a) covered the tabernacle at night
    b) at this sign, the Israelites set out on their journey
    c) at this sign, the Israelites made camp

5. When you glean a field, you
    a) sell it.
    b) gather leftover crops after the harvest.
    c) use it to bury the dead.
    d) cut down all the trees on it.

ANSWERS

1. d (1 Samuel 16:15–19)
2. gold (Exodus 25:10–14)
3. olives (Matthew 24:3; Joshua 24:13 NIV; Genesis 8:11)
4. a (Numbers 9:15–16)
5. b (Leviticus 19:9–10)

Day 9

1. Connect the Thoughts:
   Jezebel
   Elymas
   a woman of Endor

2. Complete the scripture:
   Let not sin therefore ___ in your mortal body, that ye should obey it in the lusts thereof.

3. Match: Satan's destruction. . .
   a) by another flood
   b) by fire, before the thousand-year period of peace
   c) by fire, after the thousand-year period of peace

4. What disciple, watching Jesus' arrest and trial, claimed three times that he didn't know the Lord?

5. To reach heaven, the people tried to build
   a) the Empire State Building.
   b) a highway to heaven.
   c) the Tower of Babel.
   d) the Sears Building.

ANSWERS

1. witchcraft, or sorcery (2 Kings 9:22; Acts 13:8; 1 Samuel 28:7)
2. reign (Romans 6:12 KJV)
3. c (Revelation 20:7, 9–10)
4. Peter (Matthew 26:69–75)
5. c (Genesis 11:4, 8–9)

Day 10

1. In what parable does Jesus quote, " 'My son, . . .you are always with me, and everything I have is yours' "?

2. Complete the scripture:
Train up a child in the ___ he should go: and when he is old, he will not depart from it.

3. According to the book of Romans, "there is therefore now no" *what* "to them which are in Christ Jesus"?
    a) fear of death
    b) sorrow
    c) condemnation
    d) suffering

4. When the apostle Paul wrote that "to live is Christ," what did he say it is "to die"?

5. Connect the Thoughts:
    a net
    a pearl
    a mustard seed

ANSWERS

1. the parable of the lost, or prodigal, son (Luke 15 NIV)
2. way (Proverbs 22:6 KJV)
3. c (Romans 8:1 KJV)
4. gain (Philippians 1:21 KJV)
5. objects in Jesus' parables (Matthew 13:47–50; Matthew 13:45–46; Matthew 13:31–32)

Day 11

1. What kind of bread were the Israelites to eat in their Passover celebration?

2. You can find the Ten Commandments in the following Old Testament book(s):
   a) Exodus
   b) Deuteronomy
   c) Exodus and Deuteronomy
   d) Genesis

3. Match: Gehazi. . .
   a) asked Naaman for two talents of silver.
   b) lied to Elisha and became leprous.
   c) asked Elijah for a cake of bread.

4. How many books are in the Bible?

5. The Romans were
   a) Jewish.
   b) Catholic.
   c) Gentiles.
   d) popular.

ANSWERS

1. unleavened (Numbers 9:10–11)
2. c (Exodus 20:1–17; Deuteronomy 5:7–21)
3. b (2 Kings 5:20–27)
4. sixty-six
5. c (Romans 11:13)

Day 12

1. How old was the boy Jesus when He amazed people in the temple with His spiritual insights?

2. Connect the Thoughts:
   myrrh
   frankincense
   gold

3. When does scripture say that Jesus was chosen to come to earth and offer a sacrifice for our sins?

4. Match: How Jesus as Redeemer will return. . .
   a) Jesus will come again in the clouds.
   b) An earthquake will announce Jesus' second coming.
   c) Jesus will come amid loud claps of thunder and lightning.

5. When Jesus saw the moneychangers at the temple, He
   a) bought three doves and two goats.
   b) asked for change for the vending machines.
   c) asked what time the Bible study on the book of Revelation would occur.
   d) overturned their tables and angrily rebuked them.

ANSWERS

1. twelve (Luke 2:41–52)
2. gifts for the baby Jesus (Matthew 2:1–11)
3. before the creation of the world (1 Peter 1:18–20 NIV)
4. a (Luke 21:27–28)
5. d (John 2:13–16)

Day 13

1. What third son did Eve say God gave her in place of the murdered Abel?

2. True or False: Jacob was renamed Israel.

3. Complete the scripture:
   Noah found ____ in the eyes of the LORD.

4. After Moses' death, who succeeded him?

5. We first meet Aaron in the Bible when he is
   a) a baby being hidden from Pharaoh.
   b) speaking to Pharaoh's daughter about a Hebrew nurse for Moses.
   c) writing down the Ten Commandments.
   d) appointed by God to help Moses.

ANSWERS

1. Seth (Genesis 4:1-2, 25)
2. True (Genesis 32:27–28, 35:9–10)
3. grace (Genesis 6:8 KJV)
4. Joshua, son of Nun (Deuteronomy 34:7–9)
5. d (Exodus 4:14)

Day 14

1. How many days did God use to create the world and everything in it?

2. True or False: John the Baptist begged Jesus for the privilege of baptizing Him since He is the Son of God.

3. Connect the Thoughts:
   the Shunammite's son
   Eutychus
   Lazarus

4. How many loaves of bread, along with two fish, did Jesus turn into a meal for five thousand men?

5. Match: Calming the storm. . .
   a) Jesus was piloting the boat.
   b) Jesus was having a meal.
   c) Jesus was sleeping.

ANSWERS

1. six (Genesis 1:31–2:1)
2. False (Matthew 3:13–15)
3. people raised from the dead (2 Kings 4:32–37; Acts 20:9–12; John 11:1–44)
4. five (Matthew 14:17–21)
5. c (Matthew 8:23–24)

Day 15

1. What special talent did God give to Daniel that would later help the king?

2. God promises believers
   a) earthly riches.
   b) eternal life.
   c) manna.
   d) a year's supply of Rice a Roni, the San Francisco treat.

3. What form did the Holy Spirit take when He descended on Jesus after His baptism in the Jordan River?

4. Complete the scripture:
   Create in me a clean heart, O God; and renew a ___ spirit within me.

5. What three things did God create on the fourth day to light the universe?

ANSWERS

1. understanding of visions and dreams (Daniel 1:17)
2. b (John 3:16)
3. a dove (Matthew 3:13–17)
4. right (Psalm 51:10 KJV)
5. the sun, the moon, and the stars (Genesis 1:14–19)

Day 16

1. What apostle and New Testament author was originally known as Saul?

2. True or False: John the Baptist wrote the Gospel of John.

3. What disciple betrayed Jesus with a kiss?

4. Connect the Thoughts:
   an apostle
   a tanner
   a sorcerer

5. Match: Deaths of the disciples. . .
   a) Peter drowned in the Sea of Galilee.
   b) James was martyred by King Herod.
   c) John was crucified upside down.

ANSWERS

1. Paul (Acts 13:9)
2. False. The Gospel of John is attributed to the apostle John, the son of Zebedee.
3. Judas Iscariot (Mark 14:43–45; John 6:70–71)
4. men named Simon (Matthew 10:2; Acts 9:43; Acts 8:9)
5. b (Acts 12:1–2)

Day 17

1. Where did God plant a garden and place the man, Adam, He had created?

2. Connect the Thoughts:
   Babel
   Siloam
   Jerusalem

3. What site did Abraham purchase as a family burial place?

4. King Artaxerxes found the city of Jerusalem to be
   a) peaceful.
   b) fun loving.
   c) on the cutting edge of technology.
   d) rebellious.

5. True or False: When the New Testament was written, Israel was the largest and most powerful nation on earth.

ANSWERS

1. Eden (Genesis 2:8)
2. places with towers (Genesis 11:5–9; Luke 13:4; 2 Chronicles 26:9)
3. the cave of Machpelah (Genesis 23:19)
4. d (Ezra 4:19)
5. False. Israel was no longer an independent nation but a province of a larger empire.

Day 18

1. What name, meaning "God with us," did Isaiah prophesy for Jesus?

2. Complete the scripture:
   [Jesus] bare our sins in his own body on the ____,
   that we, being dead to sins, should live unto righteousness.

3. Match: A sign Jesus is the Prince of Peace. . .
   a) A lamb without blemish was at Jesus' baptism.
   b) A dove alit on Jesus after His baptism.
   c) A rainbow appeared overhead after Jesus' baptism.

4. What did Jesus ask the woman at the well to give Him?

5. What important news did Jesus tell the woman at the well about Himself?

ANSWERS

1. Immanuel or Emmanuel (Isaiah 7:14; Matthew 1:22–23)
2. tree (1 Peter 2:24 KJV)
3. b (Matthew 3:16)
4. a drink of water (John 4:7)
5. that He is the Messiah (John 4:25–26)

Day 19

1. Unleavened bread is made
   a) without yeast.
   b) with yeast.
   c) in an oven that is off balance.
   d) by the Wonder company.

2. What product were the Israelites, as slaves of Egypt, forced to make?

3. Connect the Thoughts:
   King Ahasuerus' scepter
   a calf-shaped idol
   the streets of the new Jerusalem

4. Match: Lentil stew. . .
   a) served in the parable of the lost son
   b) served at the wedding in Cana
   c) what Jacob made Esau

5. True or False: The first bird Noah sent away from the ark was a dove.

ANSWERS

1. a (Exodus 12:20)
2. bricks (Exodus 5:4–8)
3. golden things (Esther 8:1–4; Exodus 32:2–4; Revelation 21:2, 21)
4. c (Genesis 25:34)
5. False (Genesis 8:7–8)

Day 20

1. What relationship did Abram claim to his wife, Sarai, to try to gain favor with the Egyptians?

2. Connect the Thoughts:
    Cain
    Barabbas
    the devil

3. What over-indulgers in food, according to the Proverbs, should be avoided?

4. If we say we have no sin, we are fooling
    a) ourselves.
    b) our parents.
    c) our teachers.
    d) our friends.

5. What did the Lord do when He saw that men were trying to build a tower to reach heaven?

ANSWERS

1. brother to sister (Genesis 12:10–20)
2. murderers (Genesis 4:8; Mark 15:7; John 8:44)
3. gluttons (Proverbs 23:20–21)
4. a (1 John 1:8)
5. He caused them to speak different languages and scattered them over the earth (Genesis 11:7–8).

Day 21

1. What did Jesus command His followers to show to their enemies?

2. Complete the scripture:
Work out your own salvation with fear and ___.

3. On what surface did Jesus say a wise man built his house?

4. What type of relationship did Paul tell the Galatians their salvation gave them to God "through Christ"?
   a) friends
   b) heirs
   c) students
   d) subjects

5. Match: The kingdom of heaven. . .
   a) is like a ketchup seed.
   b) is like a lost sapphire.
   c) is like yeast in dough.

ANSWERS

1. love (Luke 6:35)
2. trembling (Philippians 2:12 KJV)
3. on rock (Matthew 7:24)
4. b (Galatians 4:7 KJV)
5. c (Matthew 13:33 NIV)

Day 22

1. An epistle is a
   a) letter.
   b) book.
   c) novel.
   d) wife of an apostle.

2. What physical condition of Elisha was once mocked by young people—leading to their mauling by bears?

3. Connect the Thoughts:
   Pentecost
   Jesus walks on water
   Job's children

4. Match: King Jehoash. . .
   a) was told by Elisha to strike the ground with his arrows.
   b) struck the ground five times with his arrows, upon Elisha's instruction.
   c) was told by Elijah to strike the ground three times.

5. When the psalmist David wrote "Bless the LORD, O my soul," what three-word phrase did he remind himself to "forget not"?

ANSWERS

1. a
2. baldness (2 Kings 2:23–24)
3. strong winds (Acts 2:1–2; Matthew 14:26–32; Job 1:18–19)
4. a (2 Kings 13:14–18 NIV)
5. "all his benefits" (Psalm 103:2 KJV)

Day 23

1. How many days had Jesus fasted in the desert when Satan tempted Him to turn stones into bread?

2. What word completes Jesus' quote "Thy word is. . ."?
   a) wisdom
   b) power
   c) hope
   d) truth

3. Complete the scripture:
   Then said Jesus unto his disciples, If any man will come after me, let him ___ himself, and take up his cross, and follow me.

4. Match: Good Shepherd. . .
   a) Baby Jesus was greeted first by shepherds.
   b) Jesus was raised by Joseph, a shepherd.
   c) Many of Jesus' disciples were shepherds.

5. Who will judge all of us?

ANSWERS

1. forty (Matthew 4:1–4)
2. d (John 17:17 KJV)
3. deny (Matthew 16:24 KJV)
4. a (Luke 2:15–18)
5. Jesus Christ (Romans 14:10)

Day 24

1. Gideon's story is found in which Bible book?
   a) Judges
   b) Matthew
   c) Exodus
   d) Nehemiah

2. What Old Testament prophet once had his name changed to "Belteshazzar"?

3. Connect the Thoughts:
   Samson
   Deborah
   Ehud

4. Who does James say "believed God, and it was imputed [or credited] unto him for righteousness"?
   a) Abraham
   b) Solomon
   c) Noah
   d) Joshua

5. What prostitute urged the men of Jericho to quickly pursue two Israelite spies—while she harbored those spies in her own home?

ANSWERS

1. a (Judges 6:11–8:32)
2. Daniel (Daniel 1:7)
3. judges, or deliverers, of Israel (Judges 16:30–31 KJV; Judges 4:4 KJV; Judges 3:15)
4. a (James 2:23 KJV)
5. Rahab (Joshua 2:1–6)

Day 25

1. What disaster caused Jacob to send his sons from Canaan to Egypt?

2. Connect the Thoughts:
   David spares King Saul's life
   Obadiah hides one hundred prophets of God
   Lazarus is raised to life

3. What significant event concerning man's lifespan occurred during Noah's time?

4. Match: Walking on water. . .
   a) The apostles thought Jesus was a ghost.
   b) Peter sank to the bottom of the lake.
   c) The apostles still did not believe Jesus was the Son of God.

5. What did God take from Adam to make Eve?

ANSWERS

1. famine (Genesis 42:1–5)
2. occurrences in caves (1 Samuel 24:3–4; 1 Kings 18:4; John 11:38–44)
3. During Noah's time, the lifespan of humans was shortened to 120 years (Genesis 6:3).
4. a (Matthew 14:25–26)
5. a rib (Genesis 2:21–22)

Day 26

1. What did Jesus promise that God the Father would give to anyone who asked?

2. We can have peace with God through
   a) random acts of kindness.
   b) helping an old lady cross the street every day.
   c) making sure we give 10 percent of our allowance to church every Sunday.
   d) faith in our Lord Jesus Christ.

3. Complete the scripture:
   God is our refuge and ___, a very present help in trouble.

4. What did Hannah request of God?

5. How did God answer Hannah's prayer?

ANSWERS

1. the Holy Spirit (Luke 11:11–13)
2. d (Romans 5:1)
3. strength (Psalm 46:1 KJV)
4. She asked to give birth to a son (1 Samuel 1:9–11).
5. Hannah gave birth to a son (1 Samuel 1:20).

Day 27

1. What nickname did Jesus give to the disciple brothers James and John?

2. True or False: John was the first disciple called by Jesus.

3. Connect the Thoughts:
    John the Baptist
    James, brother of the apostle John
    Stephen

4. What was the first name of the apostle known as "the zealot" or "Zelotes" ?

5. Match: Eunice. . .
    a) mother of John Mark
    b) mother of Barnabas
    c) mother of Timothy

ANSWERS

1. Boanerges, or Sons of Thunder (Mark 3:17)
2. False. Simon (Peter) and Andrew, two fishermen brothers, were called first (Matthew 4:18–19; Mark 1:16–20).
3. martyrs (Matthew 14:3–10; Acts 12:1–2; Acts 7:59–60)
4. Simon (Luke 6:12–16)
5. c (2 Timothy 1:5)

Day 28

1. What part of the body completes the meaning of the name Golgotha: "the place of the. . ."?

2. Connect the Thoughts:
   Nebo
   Ararat
   Sinai

3. Kerith Ravine was located
   a) east of Eden.
   b) west of the Jordan.
   c) east of Jordan.
   d) near one of Michael Jordan's homes.

4. When the Israelites moved into the Promised Land, what city became the permanent home of the tabernacle?

5. What town, whose name means "house of bread," was near the site where Rachel was buried?

ANSWERS

1. skull (John 19:17 NIV)
2. mountains (Deuteronomy 34:1; Genesis 8:4; Exodus 19:20)
3. c (1 Kings 17:3 NIV)
4. Shiloh (Joshua 18:1)
5. Bethlehem (Genesis 35:19)

Day 29

1. What did Jesus and Peter pay with a coin found in a fish's mouth?

2. Jesus called Himself
   a) the manna of man.
   b) divine.
   c) the bread of life.
   d) the world's best teacher.

3. Who ministered to Jesus after His temptation in the wilderness?

4. Match: High Priest. . .
   a) Jesus was descended from the high priest Nadab.
   b) Jesus was descended from the tribe of Levi.
   c) Jesus is a high priest of the order of Melchizedek.

5. What will happen to those who say that Jesus is the Son of God?

ANSWERS

1. tax (Matthew 17:24–27)
2. c (John 6:43–48)
3. angels (Matthew 4:1, 11)
4. c (Hebrews 6:20 NIV)
5. God will live in them, and they will live in God (1 John 4:15).

Day 30

1. In the Bible, Christians are sometimes referred to as
   a) goats.
   b) vipers.
   c) serpents.
   d) sheep.

2. What two foods were said to flow in the land of Canaan?

3. Connect the Thoughts:
   grass
   a fig tree
   a man's hand

4. Match: Grapes. . .
   a) what Jael served to Sisera
   b) produce carried back from Canaan by Israel's spies
   c) what Ahab choked on

5. What two types of materials were used to make the curtains in the tabernacle?

ANSWERS

1. d (Matthew 25:31–34)
2. milk and honey (Numbers 13:17, 27)
3. things that withered (Isaiah 40:7; Matthew 21:18–19; Matthew 12:9–13)
4. b (Numbers 13:17, 23)
5. linen (Exodus 26:1) and goats' hair (Exodus 26:7)

Day 31

1. True or False: Ahab angered God more than any king of Israel before him.

2. What priests, the two sons of Eli, were judged for treating the Lord's offerings with contempt?

3. Jonah boarded a ship to Tarshish because
   a) Tarshish was on the way to Nineveh.
   b) he had been told to take a priest from Tarshish with him.
   c) he wanted to flee from the Lord.
   d) he needed a catch of fish to take along as food.

4. According to the three-part warning in the book of James, "when lust hath conceived, it bringeth forth sin: and sin, when it is finished, bringeth forth" what?

5. Eve was tempted by a
   a) serpent.
   b) ladybug.
   c) dinosaur.
   d) spider.

ANSWERS

1. True (1 Kings 16:30–33)
2. Hophni and Phinehas (1 Samuel 1:3, 2:12–17)
3. c (Jonah 1:3)
4. death (James 1:15 KJV)
5. a (Genesis 3:1)

Day 32

1. Complete the scripture:
   In the beginning was the ____, and the ____ was with God, and the ____ was God.

2. What tiny seed did Jesus liken the kingdom of heaven to?

3. John said Jesus would baptize with the Holy Ghost and with
   a) wine.
   b) fire.
   c) ashes.
   d) water.

4. What phrase completes the apostle Paul's quotation about suffering for Christ's sake: "For when I am weak. . ."?

5. Connect the Thoughts:
   honor your father and mother
   don't murder
   don't covet

ANSWERS

1. Word, Word, Word (John 1:1 KJV)
2. mustard (Matthew 13:1–3, 31–32)
3. b (Matthew 3:1, 11)
4. "then am I strong" (2 Corinthians 12:10 KJV)
5. the Ten Commandments (Exodus 20:1–17)

Day 33

1. What substance appeared on Gideon's fleece one night—but not the next—to convince him he was working in God's will?

2. Match: Hazael. . .
   a) was told by Elisha that he would die.
   b) was told by Elisha that he would be king of Judah.
   c) asked Elisha if the king of Aram would get well.

3. True or False: Although Rahab's story is recorded in the Old Testament, she is mentioned at least twice in the New Testament.

4. Connect the Thoughts:
   the father of lies
   the accuser of the brethren
   Beelzebub

5. Who wrote the Epistle to the Hebrews?

ANSWERS

1. dew (Judges 6:36–40)
2. c (2 Kings 8:9)
3. True (Hebrews 11:31; James 2:25)
4. names of Satan (John 8:44; Revelation 12:9–10 KJV; Matthew 12:24)
5. We do not know, although some Bible scholars think Paul the apostle wrote it.

Day 34

1. Match: Jesus. . .
    a) upon birth, wrapped in purple cloth by Mary
    b) upon birth, encompassed in Joseph's robes
    c) upon birth, wrapped in bands of cloth by Mary

2. What did a Simon from Cyrene carry for Jesus as He walked to His execution?

3. Complete the scripture:
    Whosoever drinketh of the water that I shall give him shall never ____.

4. Some people said Jesus was
    a) Elijah.
    b) John the Baptist.
    c) Jeremiah.
    d) all of the above.

5. True or False: Jesus approved of the process of buying and selling sacrificial doves and other animals in the temple, since it was so convenient for everyone concerned.

ANSWERS

1. c (Luke 2:7)
2. His cross (Luke 23:26)
3. thirst (John 4:14 KJV)
4. d (Matthew 16:13–14)
5. False (Mark 11:15)

Day 35

1. Which tribe of Israel had responsibility for moving the ark?

2. Rahab hid the spies
   a) on the roof of her house.
   b) at the house of a friend.
   c) in the cellar of her house.
   d) with a priest at the temple.

3. Leah's story is recorded in what book of the Bible?

4. Connect the Thoughts:
   Esther
   Jezebel
   Athaliah

5. Match: Jehoiakim. . .
   a) king who fled from the Babylonians against Jeremiah's advice
   b) king of Babylon
   c) king who burned Jeremiah's scrolls

ANSWERS

1. Levi (Deuteronomy 10:8)
2. a (Joshua 2:3–6)
3. Genesis
4. queens (Esther 2:17; 1 Kings 16:29–31; 2 Chronicles 22:10–12)
5. c (Jeremiah 36:1, 23, 27)

Day 36

1. What special celebration saw property that had been sold returned to its original owners?

2. Connect the Thoughts:
   spying in Canaan
   the sun stands still
   Jericho's walls fall

3. Match: Healing a paralyzed man. . .
   a) The man was brought in through a window.
   b) Jesus healed him without seeing him.
   c) The man was lowered through the roof.

4. How many smooth stones did David pick up to fight Goliath?

5. What did the Philistines do after David killed Goliath?

ANSWERS

1. Jubilee (Leviticus 25:28)
2. events in Joshua's life (Numbers 13:1-17; Joshua 10:13–15; Joshua 6:12–20)
3. c (Mark 2:4)
4. five (1 Samuel 17:23, 39–40)
5. They ran away (1 Samuel 17:51).

Day 37

1. What did God tell Moses he was standing on when he approached the burning bush?

2. Complete the scripture:
   O my God, I trust in thee: let me not be ___, let not mine enemies triumph over me.

3. How many times did God call Samuel before Samuel answered, "Speak; for thy servant heareth"?

4. When God spoke to Samuel, Samuel thought he was being called by
   a) Eli.
   b) Hannah.
   c) an angel.
   d) the alien E.T.

5. The Lord told Samuel He planned to
   a) bless Eli.
   b) bless Eli's sons.
   c) allow Eli to win a dream house in a raffle.
   d) punish Eli's house because Eli's sons were evil.

ANSWERS

1. holy ground (Exodus 3:3–5)
2. ashamed (Psalm 25:2 KJV)
3. Samuel answered the Lord on the fourth call (1 Samuel 3:8–10 KJV).
4. a (1 Samuel 3:5)
5. d (1 Samuel 3:11–14)

Day 38

1. What Caesar ordered the census that brought Mary, expecting the baby Jesus, to Bethlehem?

2. What early Christian leader explained the way of salvation to an Ethiopian eunuch, who accepted Christ, was baptized, and "went on his way rejoicing"?
   a) Philip
   b) Andrew
   c) Nathanael
   d) Apollos

3. What physical characteristic initially hindered Zacchaeus from seeing Jesus?

4. Connect the Thoughts:
   missionary companion of the apostle Paul
   correspondent with Theophilus
   beloved physician

5. True or False: Paul was in prison when he wrote to Philemon.

ANSWERS

1. Augustus (Luke 2:1–5)
2. a (Acts 8:26–39 KJV)
3. shortness (Luke 19:3)
4. Luke (2 Timothy 4:11; Luke 1:3; Colossians 4:14)
5. True (Philemon 1:1)

Day 39

1. What mountain, where Moses received the Ten Commandments, shook as the Lord came down on it?

2. Connect the Thoughts:
    Pharpar
    Pison
    Jordan

3. In what city did silversmiths—fearing the effect of Paul's preaching on their idol-making business—stir up a riot?

4. Match: Tyre. . .
    a) where Peter restored Tabitha to life
    b) where Jesus restored a widow's son to life
    c) where Jesus healed a demon-possessed girl

5. Where will the ark of the covenant ultimately be found?

ANSWERS

1. Mount Sinai (Exodus 19:18–19)
2. rivers (2 Kings 5:12; Genesis 2:10–11; Mark 1:5)
3. Ephesus (Acts 19:24–32)
4. c (Matthew 15:21–28)
5. in heaven (Revelation 11:19)

Day 40

1. What town in Galilee was the boyhood home of Jesus?

2. Match: Jesus. . .
   a) After His crucifixion, His clothes were given back to Mary.
   b) Peter asked the soldiers for Jesus' clothes.
   c) He wore a seamless undergarment.

3. True or False: Joseph and Mary reared Jesus as a Christian.

4. Who asked Jesus to perform His first miracle?
   a) Joseph
   b) Mary
   c) Elijah
   d) a nervous bridegroom

5. True or False: Since it was important that Jesus not damage His reputation as God's Son, He avoided associating with outcasts and sinners while here on earth.

ANSWERS

1. Nazareth (Matthew 2:19–23)
2. c (John 19:23 NIV)
3. False. Jesus was reared in the Jewish faith. Christianity was not established until after Jesus' resurrection.
4. b (John 2:3)
5. False (Mark 2:15)

Day 41

1. Noah sent a dove out of the ark
   a) to see if the waters had gone down so they could leave the ark.
   b) to find Dove Bars because they were hungry.
   c) to dig up some worms for the other birds on the ark.
   d) to symbolize peace in the world.

2. What did the fearful Israelite spies who explored Canaan say they looked like compared to the giants they saw there?

3. Connect the Thoughts:
   shekel
   talent
   pound

4. Match: Fish. . .
   a) what Jesus served some disciples for breakfast
   b) created on the fourth day
   c) created on the third day

5. True or False: Noah waited seven days between each time he sent the dove out from the ark.

ANSWERS

1. a (Genesis 8:1, 8)
2. grasshoppers (Numbers 13:17, 33)
3. measurements of weight (Genesis 24:22; 2 Samuel 12:30; John 19:39)
4. a (John 21:4–13)
5. True (Genesis 8:10, 12)

Day 42

1. What did the apostle Paul say "dwelleth in me" and caused him to struggle spiritually?
   a) evil
   b) carnality
   c) falsehood
   d) sin

2. What husband and wife died after lying about the amount of money they gave as an offering?

3. If Eve would eat the forbidden fruit, the serpent promised her
   a) clothing.
   b) riches.
   c) a starring role in a movie.
   d) knowledge of good and evil.

4. Why did God reject Saul as king?

5. What unaccepted offering provoked Cain's murder of Abel?

ANSWERS

1. d (Romans 7:15–17 KJV)
2. Ananias and Sapphira (Acts 5:1–11)
3. d (Genesis 3:1, 5)
4. Because Saul disobeyed God (1 Samuel 15:20–23)
5. fruits of the soil (Genesis 4:3–5 NIV)

Day 43

1. What did Jesus say was more likely to go through the eye of a needle than for a rich man to enter heaven?

2. What follows "In all thy ways acknowledge him" in a beloved passage of Proverbs?
   a) "and he shall direct thy paths."
   b) "and he shall sustain thee."
   c) "and he shall hear thy prayers."
   d) "and he shall vindicate thee."

3. Instead of suing your enemy and taking him to court, what course of action did Jesus advise?

4. Complete the scripture:
   For by grace are ye saved through ___; and that not of yourselves: it is the gift of God.

5. Match: The lost son. . .
   a) The father gave his lost son a ring and sandals.
   b) The father gave his lost son a chariot and horses.
   c) The father gave his lost son a vineyard.

ANSWERS

1. a camel (Matthew 19:23–24)
2. a (Proverbs 3:6 KJV)
3. settling matters out of court (Matthew 5:25)
4. faith (Ephesians 2:8 KJV)
5. a (Luke 15:21–22)

Day 44

1. What does the "lover" in the Song of Solomon twice compare his "beloved's" hair to?

2. A Pharisee was a
   a) civil servant.
   b) university teacher.
   c) doctor of the law.
   d) tax collector.

3. What did Jacob wear to make his father, whose eyes were dim with age, think he was hairy like Esau?

4. Connect the Thoughts:
   Jesus' disciples
   tribes of Israel
   gates of the new Jerusalem

5. Name at least two people of faith described in Hebrews.

ANSWERS

1. a flock of goats (Song of Solomon 4:1, 6:5)
2. c (Acts 5:34 KJV)
3. the skins of goat kids (Genesis 27:15–16)
4. twelve (Matthew 10:1; Genesis 49:28; Revelation 21:2, 21)
5. Abel, Enoch, Noah, Abraham, Sarah, Isaac, Jacob, Joseph, the parents of Moses, Moses, Rahab (Hebrews 11)

Day 45

1. What "Mount of" was frequented by Jesus?

2. Match: Jesus. . .
   a) fasted before being baptized by John the Baptist.
   b) fasted before choosing His disciples.
   c) fasted before meeting Satan.

3. Who saw Satan fall as lightning from heaven?

4. What color horse does Jesus ride during the great battle in the book of Revelation?
   a) gold
   b) red
   c) white
   d) black

5. What door-openers to the kingdom of heaven did Jesus say He would give to Peter?

ANSWERS

1. Olives (Luke 22:39)
2. c (Matthew 4:2–3)
3. Jesus (Luke 10:1–2, 17–18)
4. c (Revelation 19:11)
5. keys (Matthew 16:15–19)

Day 46

1. What evil woman led Israel's King Ahab, her husband, into Baal worship?

2. What king of Judah "trusted in the LORD God of Israel" —and was rewarded with an extra fifteen years of life?
   a) Hezekiah
   b) Manasseh
   c) Asa
   d) Jehoshaphat

3. What job did the youthful David have before his anointing as king?

4. Connect the Thoughts:
   a dove
   a rainbow
   the mountains of Ararat

5. Match: Jotham. . .
   a) proclaimed himself king of Shechem.
   b) was the only brother to escape Abimelech's wrath.
   c) was the last judge of Israel.

ANSWERS

1. Jezebel (1 Kings 16:29–31)
2. a (2 Kings 18:1–5, 20:1–6 KJV)
3. shepherd (1 Samuel 16:11–13)
4. the story of Noah and the ark (Genesis 8:8–9; Genesis 9:16–17; Genesis 8:1–4)
5. b (Judges 9:4–5)

Day 47

1. What illegal activity resulted in Daniel being thrown into the lions' den?

2. Connect the Thoughts:
   at Cana in Galilee
   of the Lamb
   Jesus' parable of a king and his son

3. Match: Fiery furnace. . .
   a) Shadrach, Meshach, and Abednego wore only trousers in the furnace.
   b) King Nebuchadnezzar ordered the furnace seven times hotter.
   c) King Nebuchadnezzar saw five men inside the furnace.

4. Match: Esther. . .
   a) held a triathlon to see who would be her king.
   b) won a beauty contest and married the king.
   c) paid the king a lot of money to marry her because she was ugly.
   d) was not Jewish.

5. From which tribe was King Saul?

ANSWERS

1. praying to God (Daniel 6:6–14)
2. weddings (John 2:1; Revelation 19:7; Matthew 22:1–2)
3. b (Daniel 3:19)
4. b (Esther 2:5–17)
5. the tribe of Benjamin (1 Samuel 9:16)

Day 48

1. What storm-related phenomenon is likened to God's voice in the books of Job and John?

2. The Lord told Samuel to
   a) let the people see how a king would rule.
   b) sacrifice two goats and a perfect male ram.
   c) produce two more sons more worthy to be judges.
   d) store grain for seven years because there would be seven years of famine.

3. When the people asked for a king, whom did the Lord say they were really rejecting?

4. When we pray, whose plan shall be carried out?
   a) ours
   b) God's
   c) our pastor's
   d) our parents'

5. Who is in charge of seeking revenge for evil?

ANSWERS

1. thunder (Job 37:4–5; John 12:23–29)
2. a (1 Samuel 8:9)
3. the Lord Himself (1 Samuel 8:7)
4. b (Romans 8:27)
5. God (Romans 12:19)

Day 49

1. What man, with a name like a Roman god, became a powerful preacher of Christ in the early church?

2. The Pharisees believed in
   a) life after death and the supernatural.
   b) life after death, but not angels.
   c) neither life after death nor the supernatural.
   d) angels, but not in life after death.

3. What disciple found himself "weightless" enough to walk on water with Jesus—only as long as he kept his focus on the Lord?

4. Connect the Thoughts:
   locusts
   camel's hair
   wild honey

5. True or False: Mary Magdalene is mentioned in all four Gospels.

ANSWERS

1. Apollos (Acts 18:24–26)
2. a (Acts 23:6–9)
3. Peter (Matthew 14:28–31)
4. John the Baptist (Matthew 3:1, 4)
5. True (Matthew 27:56; Mark 15:40; Luke 8:2; John 19:25)

Day 50

1. Where did God tell Isaac's father to sacrifice the young man as a burnt offering?

2. In what city did Silas and Paul—the former persecutor Saul—lead the local jailer to life in Christ?
   a) Troas
   b) Berea
   c) Philippi
   d) Athens

3. How many days would it take a person to walk through the city of Nineveh?

4. Match: Valley of Ben Hinnom. . .
   a) also known as Valley of Hope
   b) also known as Topheth
   c) also known as Valley of Despair

5. When the Israelites camped in the wilderness, on what side of the tabernacle did the tribes of Judah, Zebulun, and Issachar camp together?

ANSWERS

1. Moriah (Genesis 22:1–2)
2. c (Acts 16:19–34)
3. three (Jonah 3:3)
4. b (Jeremiah 19:6 NIV)
5. east (Numbers 2:1–9)

Day 51

1. What, according to the prophet Isaiah, would Jesus carry on His shoulders?

2. Match: Jesus. . .
   a) said to fast as the Pharisees did.
   b) said to put oil on your head and wash your face.
   c) said not to fast.

3. When the Pharisees brought a woman to Jesus who was caught committing adultery, what did Jesus do first?

4. True or False: When Jesus drove demons from people, the demons proclaimed that Jesus was God's Son.

5. What did Jesus tell church members in Laodicea He would do with them if they opened the door to His knocking?

ANSWERS

1. the government (Isaiah 9:6)
2. b (Matthew 5:1, 6:17)
3. He bent down and started writing on the ground with His finger (John 8:4–6).
4. True (Luke 4:41)
5. eat with them (Revelation 3:14, 20)

Day 52

1. What did the angels who visited Sodom do with Lot?

2. What vegetable did the complaining Israelites recall from their years of slavery in Egypt?

3. Connect the Thoughts:
   when Rebekah met Isaac
   straining out gnats
   the eye of a needle

4. Match: Vegetables. . .
   a) Daniel's diet for ten days
   b) Esther's beauty secret
   c) what Ruth picked in Boaz's fields

5. What animal saw the angel of the Lord?

ANSWERS

1. They brought him and his family out of Sodom and told him to flee (Genesis 19:1, 16, 22).
2. cucumbers (Numbers 11:4–5)
3. a camel (Genesis 24:64; Matthew 23:24; Luke 18:25)
4. a (Daniel 1:11–12 NIV)
5. Balaam's donkey (Numbers 22:23)

Day 53

1. What color is used to describe sin in the book of Isaiah?

2. According to Jesus, what was Satan "from the beginning"?
   a) a deceiver
   b) a rebel
   c) an enemy
   d) a murderer

3. What was the method of execution for a man who blasphemed the Lord's name with a curse?

4. True or False: God said Israel will be punished for her sins.

5. After they had sinned, what did Adam and Eve do when they heard God calling?

ANSWERS

1. crimson or scarlet (Isaiah 1:18)
2. d (John 8:44)
3. stoning (Leviticus 24:10–23)
4. True (Hosea 8:1–14)
5. They hid themselves (Genesis 3:8).

Day 54

1. What did Paul tell Timothy that Christians should lift up in prayer?

2. What did the apostle Paul say he had learned, "in whatsoever state I am"?
   a) to be content
   b) always to pray
   c) God is good
   d) faith is sufficient

3. True or False: Paul always described himself in his letters as head of the church.

4. Complete the scripture:
   Let us therefore come boldly unto the ___ of grace, that we may obtain mercy, and find grace to help in time of need.

5. Match: The rich fool. . .
   a) The rich fool wanted to tear down his barns.
   b) A famine had destroyed the rich fool's crops.
   c) The rich fool lived to be 108 years old.

ANSWERS

1. holy hands (1 Timothy 2:8)
2. a (Philippians 4:11 KJV)
3. False. He referred to himself as a servant of Christ/servant of God (Romans 1:1; Titus 1:1).
4. throne (Hebrews 4:16 KJV)
5. a (Luke 12:16–20)

Day 55

1. Who wrote the second to last book of the New Testament?

2. What did John call the new Jerusalem he saw in a vision, coming down out of heaven?

3. God instructed Noah to make the ark
    a) 300 cubits long, 50 cubits wide, and 30 cubits high.
    b) 400 cubits long, 50 cubits wide, and 60 cubits high.
    c) 300 cubits long, 50 cubits wide, and 60 cubits high.
    d) 400 cubits long, 30 cubits wide, and 30 cubits high.

4. Connect the Thoughts:
    Joseph
    the ancient Israelites
    Onesimus

5. How many books are in the Old Testament?

ANSWERS

1. Jude
2. the Holy City (Revelation 21:1–2)
3. a (Genesis 6:15)
4. slaves (Genesis 39:1–3; Exodus 2:23; Philemon 10–16)
5. thirty-nine

Day 56

1. Who did Jesus say He was calling to repentance when Pharisees asked why He ate with disreputable people?

2. What word described the crowd's response when Jesus used His authority to drive out evil spirits?

3. Match: Jesus. . .
   a) buried in a tomb with the patriarchs
   b) buried in Bethlehem
   c) buried in a garden tomb near the site of His crucifixion

4. What short word, meaning "trouble," did Jesus pronounce on the Pharisees seven times in one speech?

5. What did Jesus say a man could forfeit, negating the gain of "the whole world"?

ANSWERS

1. sinners (Matthew 9:10–13)
2. amazed (Mark 1:23–27 NIV)
3. c (John 19:41)
4. woe (Matthew 23:13–32 NIV)
5. his soul (Mark 8:36)

Day 57

1. What prophet of God challenged 450 prophets of Baal to see whose god would answer by fire?

2. What prophet resisted the temptation to accept money for healing the leper Naaman—then condemned his own servant to leprosy for taking Naaman's money dishonestly?
   a) Samuel
   b) Elijah
   c) Elisha
   d) Obadiah

3. What was Ruth doing the first time she saw Boaz, the man she would marry?

4. True or False: King Ahab was a wise ruler who worshiped Jehovah.

5. Connect the Thoughts:
   a favored son
   a dream of supremacy
   a coat of many colors

ANSWERS

1. Elijah (1 Kings 18:22–24)
2. c (2 Kings 5:1–27)
3. gleaning (Ruth 2:2–8)
4. False (1 Kings 16:29–33)
5. Joseph (Genesis 37:3; Genesis 37:5–7; Genesis 37:3)

Day 58

1. What collapsed and killed eighteen people in a "news event" that Jesus used to encourage repentance?

2. After the Flood, the Bible says that Noah
   a) planted a vegetable garden.
   b) planted a vineyard.
   c) bred goats and sheep.
   d) divided the land equally between his three sons.

3. Connect the Thoughts:
   the creation
   the fall of man
   the calling of Abraham

4. Match: Water from the rock. . .
   a) Aaron struck the rock at Horeb.
   b) Moses called the place "Meribah" because the people were happy.
   c) Moses struck the rock at Horeb.

5. True or False: The Feast of Unleavened Bread was established by God.

ANSWERS

1. a tower (Luke 13:2–5)
2. b (Genesis 8:15–18, 9:20)
3. events in the book of Genesis (Genesis 1–2:4; Genesis 3:17–19; Genesis 12:1–3)
4. c (Exodus 17:3–6)
5. True (Exodus 12:1, 17)

Day 59

1. Who is the Counselor that Jesus says He will ask the Father to give His followers?

2. The book of Job relates how
   a) to get a good job.
   b) God protects and rewards those who love Him.
   c) to cover up those ugly sores.
   d) friends help out when the going gets tough.

3. What does God think of good works done in His name?

4. True or False: We can pray to God anytime.

5. When we pray to God, we should first
   a) praise Him.
   b) ask for whatever we want.
   c) ask for good weather.
   d) tell Him we haven't done anything wrong.

ANSWERS

1. the Holy Spirit (John 14:16–17)
2. b (Job 42:12–17)
3. He will not forget them (Hebrews 6:10).
4. True. God listens to us any time of the day or night (Luke 18: 1-8).
5. a (Luke 11:2)

Day 60

1. John says he wrote his book so you will
   a) feed the poor.
   b) be healthy, wealthy, and wise.
   c) be a good person.
   d) believe in Jesus Christ, the Son of God, and have life in His name.

2. What "prickly" physical ailment did Paul write about to the church at Corinth?

3. Felix was governor of
   a) Judea.
   b) Caesarea.
   c) Jerusalem.
   d) Rome.

4. Match: Ephraim. . .
   a) younger son of Joseph
   b) forefather of Jesus
   c) firstborn son of Joseph

5. King Herod sought the baby Jesus to
   a) worship Him.
   b) give Him gold, frankincense, and myrrh.
   c) give Mary and Joseph money for a hotel room.
   d) kill Him.

ANSWERS

1. d (John 20:31)
2. a thorn in the flesh (2 Corinthians 12:7)
3. b (Acts 23:23–24)
4. a (Genesis 48:8–20)
5. d (Matthew 2:13)

Day 61

1. What city's walls fell at the shout of Joshua's army?

2. Rahab's house was located
   a) on a mountaintop.
   b) on the town wall.
   c) near a grape arbor
   d) just behind the entrance to the city.

3. What mount approximately five miles from Nazareth is reputed to be the traditional site of the Transfiguration?

4. Match: Beersheba. . .
   a) where Naaman was healed of leprosy
   b) where Samuel was raised in the temple
   c) where Elijah fled to escape Jezebel

5. What tribes of Israel settled east of the Jordan River?

ANSWERS

1. Jericho (Joshua 6:2–5, 20)
2. b (Joshua 2:3, 15)
3. Mt. Tabor
4. c (1 Kings 19:1–3)
5. Gad, Reuben, and Manasseh (Joshua 18:7)

Day 62

1. What Greek letter did Jesus pair with "Alpha" to describe Himself?

2. Match: Jesus. . .
   a) buried by Roman soldiers with guidance from the disciples
   b) buried by Joseph and Nicodemus
   c) buried by Mary and Mary Magdalene

3. What two commands on prayer, besides "knock," did Jesus give during His Sermon on the Mount?

4. Complete the verse:
   Heaven and earth shall ___ ___: but my words shall not ___ ___.

5. When Jesus said, "No man cometh unto the Father, but by me," what two names did He give Himself besides "the life"?

ANSWERS

1. Omega (Revelation 22:12–13)
2. b (John 19:38–42)
3. ask and seek (Matthew 5:1, 7:7–8)
4. pass away, pass away (Luke 21:33 KJV)
5. the way, the truth (John 14:6 KJV)

Day 63

1. What insects are mentioned by the writer of the book of James as destroyers of clothing?

2. Connect the Thoughts:
   the wise men and Jesus
   Wormwood
   the fourth day of creation

3. Match: Nehemiah. . .
   a) was a scribe for Cyrus in Jerusalem.
   b) kept the ark of the covenant in Jerusalem for David.
   c) rebuilt Jerusalem's walls after captivity.

4. What kind of tree supplied the wood for Aaron's rod that budded?

5. What metals did Tubalcain work with?

ANSWERS

1. moths (James 5:2)
2. stars (Matthew 2:1–2; Revelation 8:10–11; Genesis 1:16–19)
3. c (Nehemiah 1:3, 6:15)
4. almond (Numbers 17:8)
5. brass and iron (Genesis 4:22)

Day 64

1. How did Jesus instruct Judas Iscariot to do his evil work of betrayal?

2. When he was caught disobeying God, Adam blamed
   a) the serpent.
   b) bad programs on television.
   c) Cain.
   d) Eve.

3. Who convinced a prophet to sin by claiming he had a message from the angel of the Lord?

4. When he heard what Gehazi had done, Elisha
   a) rewarded him with half the money.
   b) complimented Gehazi on how smart he was.
   c) gave him a bigger Christmas bonus than usual for his efforts.
   d) said that Gehazi and his family would always be plagued with leprosy.

5. What two sons of Aaron were burned to death for offering unauthorized fire to the Lord?

ANSWERS

1. quickly (John 13:26–27)
2. d (Genesis 3:12)
3. an old prophet who lived in Bethel (1 Kings 13:1–22)
4. d (2 Kings 5:25–27)
5. Nadab and Abihu (Leviticus 10:1–2)

Day 65

1. A good woman is
   a) virtuous.
   b) beautiful.
   c) rich.
   d) skinny.

2. What group of people, whom the disciples tried to keep from Jesus, did Jesus say are true possessors of the kingdom of heaven?

3. Complete the scripture:
   God resisteth the proud, but giveth grace unto the ____.

4. What, according to Peter, should Christians "be ready always to give" regarding "a reason of the hope that is in you"?

5. Match: The vineyard workers. . .
   a) The last vineyard workers were hired at the eleventh hour.
   b) The vineyard workers hired first received two denarii.
   c) The first vineyard workers were hired at the sixth hour.

ANSWERS

1. a (Proverbs 31:10 KJV)
2. little children (Matthew 19:14)
3. humble (James 4:6 KJV)
4. an answer (1 Peter 3:15 KJV)
5. a (Matthew 20:1–9)

Day 66

1. What "skill" did a young slave girl lose when Paul cast a demon from her?

2. Connect the Thoughts:
   Saul and Abner
   Mordecai and Esther
   Mary and Elizabeth

3. What kind of stone, according to the apostle Paul, did God lay in Zion?

4. Match: One hundred fifty-three. . .
   a) prophets of Baal who opposed Elijah
   b) number of fish once caught by seven disciples
   c) age of Sarah when she died

5. What did Boaz buy on behalf of Naomi and Ruth?

ANSWERS

1. fortune-telling (Acts 16:16–19)
2. cousins (1 Samuel 14:49–50; Esther 2:5, 7; Luke 1:34–36)
3. stumbling (Romans 9:32–33)
4. b (John 21:2–11)
5. the property that had belonged to Naomi's sons and husband (Ruth 4:1–9)

Day 67

1. What did Jesus write in the sand when a woman was brought before Him and accused of adultery?

2. Match: Jesus. . .
   a) wept over the future destruction of Jerusalem.
   b) wept when He saw John the Baptist.
   c) is never recorded as weeping in the Bible.

3. What repetitive phrase, according to Jesus, will not guarantee entry into the kingdom of heaven?

4. What Old Testament prophet's writing did Jesus read aloud in the Nazareth synagogue, telling the people, "This day is this scripture fulfilled in your ears"?
   a) Ezekiel
   b) Esaias, or Isaiah
   c) Hosea
   d) Jeremy, or Jeremiah

5. What did Jesus once say that scripture cannot be?

ANSWERS

1. The Bible doesn't tell us what He wrote (John 8:6).
2. a (Luke 19:28, 39–44)
3. Lord, Lord (Matthew 7:21)
4. b (Luke 4:16–21)
5. broken (John 10:34–35)

Day 68

1. What "wild donkey of a man's" birth was foretold to his mother, Hagar?

2. Hannah's story takes place in
   a) 2 Samuel.
   b) 1 Chronicles.
   c) 1 Samuel.
   d) 2 Chronicles.

3. What miracle son was Abraham willing to sacrifice, "accounting that God was able to raise him up, even from the dead"?

4. Connect the Thoughts:
   lost donkeys
   a tall man
   anointing oil

5. Match: Baruch. . .
   a) wrote Jeremiah's words on a scroll.
   b) with Deborah, was a judge of Israel.
   c) accompanied Paul on his first missionary journey.

ANSWERS

1. Ishmael (Genesis 16:7–12 NIV)
2. c
3. Isaac (Hebrews 11:17–19 KJV)
4. King Saul (1 Samuel 9:3; 1 Samuel 10:21–23; 1 Samuel 10:1, 20–24)
5. a (Jeremiah 36:4)

Day 69

1. What group of people, according to Luke, received the angels' announcement of the birth of Jesus?

2. Match: Floating axhead. . .
   a) To retrieve it, Elisha threw a stick in the Jordan.
   b) To retrieve it, Gehazi jumped into the Jordan and drowned.
   c) To retrieve it, Elijah threw his cloak in the water.

3. What miracle did Peter perform in Joppa that spread Jesus' name in that city?

4. The Feast of Unleavened Bread was celebrated to remember
   a) not to run out of yeast.
   b) that man does not live by bread alone.
   c) how God brought the Israelites out of Egypt.
   d) that Jesus is the Messiah.

5. True or False: The Feast of Harvest celebrated the firstfruits of the harvest, and the Feast of Ingathering was celebrated at the end of the year.

ANSWERS

1. shepherds (Luke 2:8–15)
2. a (2 Kings 6:5–6)
3. He raised Dorcas, also known as Tabitha, from the dead (Acts 9:36–40).
4. c (Exodus 12:17)
5. True (Exodus 23:16)

Day 70

1. Complete the scripture:
God is a _____: and they that worship him must worship him in spirit and in truth.

2. The Lord told Samuel that people see outward beauty, but He sees their
a) intelligence.
b) possessions.
c) time put in at Bible study class.
d) hearts.

3. Who is the giver of wisdom?

4. To please God, a Christian must have
a) given up chocolate for Lent.
b) a long list of good deeds.
c) self-denial.
d) faith.

5. How does John define God?

ANSWERS

1. Spirit (John 4:24 KJV)
2. d (1 Samuel 16:7)
3. the Lord (Proverbs 2:6)
4. d (Hebrews 11:6)
5. God is love (1 John 4:8).

Day 71

1. What man, for whom a New Testament book is named, traveled to Corinth to help pick up an offering for needy saints?

2. Paul was sent to Felix by
   a) Claudius Lysias, a Roman soldier.
   b) King Agrippa.
   c) Caesar.
   d) Porcius Festus, Roman governor of Antioch.

3. What elderly prophetess met Mary, Joseph, and the baby Jesus at the temple and thanked God for the redemption to come?

4. Match: Dorcas. . .
   a) dealer in purple cloth
   b) known for her handmade robes
   c) made robes for Peter

5. Who wrote the Epistle to the Romans?

ANSWERS

1. Titus (2 Corinthians 8:16–19)
2. a (Acts 23:24–26)
3. Anna (Luke 2:27, 36–38)
4. b (Acts 9:39)
5. Paul the Apostle

Day 72

1. What field was purchased by the chief priests with the "blood money" they got back from a remorseful Judas Iscariot?

2. Connect the Thoughts:
    liars and evil beasts
    the harbor of Phenice (Phoenix)
    Titus' parish

3. Match: Ramah. . .
    a) where Elisha trapped blinded Arameans
    b) where Samuel was born
    c) where Elijah went up to heaven in a whirlwind

4. Who was Isaac's favorite son?

5. As the book of Acts concludes, where in Rome is the apostle Paul?
    a) Caesar's palace
    b) a dungeon
    c) the Forum
    d) a rented house

ANSWERS

1. the potter's field (Matthew 27:3–7)
2. Crete (Titus 1:12; Acts 27:12; Titus 1:5)
3. b (1 Samuel 1:19–20)
4. Esau (Genesis 25:28)
5. d (Acts 28:30)

Day 73

1. What did Jesus say He would arrive in when He returns to earth "with power and great glory"?

2. What phrase, according to Matthew's Gospel, did Jesus repeat three times while battling Satan's temptation in the wilderness?
   a) "Thou shalt not. . ."
   b) "Get thee behind me"
   c) "Woe unto ye"
   d) "It is written"

3. How many people lived in Nineveh in Jonah's time?

4. Match: Jesus. . .
   a) stood on the highest point of the temple in Jerusalem.
   b) refused Satan's offer to stand on the highest point of the temple in Jerusalem.
   c) chose His disciples outside the temple in Jerusalem.

5. How did Jesus say He came to provide life for His sheep?

ANSWERS

1. a cloud (Luke 21:27)
2. d (Matthew 4:3–10 KJV)
3. more than 120,000 (Jonah 4:11 NIV)
4. a (Luke 4:8–9)
5. more abundantly, or to the full (John 10:7–10)

Day 74

1. What was the composition of the feet of an enormous statue in King Nebuchadnezzar's dream—explained by Daniel?

2. Connect the Thoughts:
   two mites
   two pigeons
   five loaves and two fish

3. What creature of the wilderness does Malachi describe as laying waste to Esau's heritage?

4. Match: Figs. . .
   a) what Naboth grew in his orchard
   b) what God showed Jeremiah in two baskets
   c) what Eve gave to Adam

5. What job was given to cherubims after the expulsion of Adam and Eve from Eden?

ANSWERS

1. iron and clay (Daniel 2:1, 32–33)
2. small offerings to God (Mark 12:41–44 KJV; Leviticus 5:7; John 6:5–9)
3. dragons (Malachi 1:3)
4. b (Jeremiah 24:1)
5. guardians of Eden and the tree of life (Genesis 3:24)

Day 75

1. Who paid Judas Iscariot to betray Jesus?

2. After Adam and Eve ate the forbidden fruit, God
   a) sent them out of Eden.
   b) let them stay in Eden.
   c) poured manna from heaven.
   d) told them to build an ark so He could begin the human race again.

3. What was cursed by God because of Adam?

4. Egypt and Edom will be punished for attacking
   a) the United States.
   b) Saudi Arabia.
   c) Jordan.
   d) Judah.

5. Who is the angel of the bottomless pit, whose name means "the destroyer," in the book of Revelation?

ANSWERS

1. the chief priests (Matthew 26:14–16)
2. a (Genesis 3:6, 22–24)
3. the ground (Genesis 3:17)
4. d (Joel 3:19)
5. Abaddon or Apollyon (Revelation 9:11)

Day 76

1. According to the book of Romans, how did God prove His love for sinners?
   a) Noah's rainbow
   b) Christ's death
   c) Paul's conversion
   d) John's Revelation

2. What two groups, according to Jesus in the Beatitudes, would inherit the kingdom of heaven?

3. Complete the scripture:
   We walk by faith, not by ____.

4. On what surface did Jesus say a foolish man built his house?

5. Match: The king's ten servants. . .
   a) The servant who earned five more minas took charge of five vineyards.
   b) The servant who earned ten more minas took charge of ten cities.
   c) The king's subjects went into mourning when the king left.

ANSWERS

1. b (Romans 5:8)
2. the poor in spirit, those persecuted for righteousness' sake (Matthew 5:1, 3, 10)
3. sight (2 Corinthians 5:7 KJV)
4. on sand (Matthew 7:26)
5. b (Luke 19:11–26)

Day 77

1. True or False: Most of the Old Testament was originally written in the Hebrew language.

2. What special headwear will be the heavenly reward for faithful service on earth?

3. Connect the Thoughts:
   King David
   Moses
   Asaph

4. How old was Noah when God sent the flood to destroy the earth?

5. Match: Micah. . .
   a) son of Tekoa
   b) the shortest book of the minor prophets
   c) foretelling of a ruler to come from Bethlehem

ANSWERS

1. True
2. a crown (2 Timothy 4:8; James 1:12)
3. authors of Psalms (Psalm 3 NIV; Psalm 90 NIV; Psalm 73 NIV)
4. six hundred years old (Genesis 7:11)
5. c (Micah 5:2)

Day 78

1. In what kind of room did Jesus celebrate His last Passover with His disciples?

2. Connect the Thoughts:
   Wonderful
   Counsellor
   The Prince of Peace

3. Match: Jesus. . .
   a) promised rest for our souls.
   b) promised great material wealth to all believers.
   c) promised salvation based on good works alone.

4. What did Jesus say His love for Christians would be like?
   a) a man with his son
   b) a shepherd with his sheep
   c) a king with his queen
   d) a bear with her cub

5. What three-word title, later applied to Jesus Christ, did the voice of God use to address the prophet Ezekiel?

ANSWERS

1. an upper room (Mark 14:12–15)
2. Isaiah's prophecy of Christ (Isaiah 9:6)
3. a (Matthew 11:28)
4. b (John 10:14)
5. son of man (Ezekiel 2:1; Matthew 8:20)

Day 79

1. What colorful garment did Joseph's father make for him?

2. Hannah named her son Samuel because
   a) she had promised the Lord she would.
   b) she had asked the Lord for him.
   c) she was told by God in a vision what to name him.
   d) Eli said that Samuel should be the boy's name.

3. What are the better-known names of Daniel's friends Hananiah, Mishael, and Azariah?

4. Samson's story can be found in
   a) The Acts of the Apostles.
   b) Judges.
   c) 2 Kings.
   d) 2 Chronicles.

5. Connect the Thoughts:
   Cyrus
   Darius
   Artaxerxes

ANSWERS

1. a coat of many colors (Genesis 37:3)
2. b (1 Samuel 1:20)
3. Shadrach, Meshach, and Abednego (Daniel 1:7)
4. b
5. kings of Persia (Ezra 1:1; Ezra 4:5; Ezra 7:1)

Day 80

1. What did Jesus, in His first recorded miracle, change into wine?

2. Match: Creation. . .
   a) On the fourth day God filled the water with fish.
   b) On the third day God created sky as separate from water.
   c) On the third day God called the waters "seas."

3. True or False: Mary Magdalene was present at the crucifixion of Jesus Christ.

4. From what punishment did God save Daniel's three friends who refused to worship Nebuchadnezzar's statue?
   a) the lions' den
   b) forty lashes
   c) the fiery furnace
   d) drawing and quartering

5. Connect the Thoughts:
   water turned to blood
   dust turned to lice
   ashes turned to boils

ANSWERS

1. water (John 2:1–11)
2. c (Genesis 1:10, 13)
3. True (Matthew 27:50, 55–56)
4. c (Daniel 3:8–25)
5. plagues on Egypt (Exodus 7:14–19; Exodus 8:16–17;Exodus 9:8–12)

Day 81

1. God corrects us because He
    a) will benefit.
    b) wants all Christians to be missionaries to the North Pole.
    c) wants us to learn how to be holy.
    d) thinks it is fun.

2. Fill in the blank:
Jesus also calls the Counselor the Spirit of ____.

3. What did the Lord tell Samuel to do when Samuel saw David?

4. We can be separated from God's love by
    a) not going to church every Wednesday and Sunday.
    b) bad people.
    c) too much television.
    d) nothing.

5. What does the writer of Hebrews say we should continually offer to God?

ANSWERS

1. c (Hebrews 12:10)
2. truth (John 16:13)
3. The Lord told Samuel to anoint David king (1 Samuel 16:11–13).
4. d (Romans 8:35–39)
5. praise (Hebrews 13:15)

Day 82

1. Who wrote the epistles to the Thessalonians?

2. What occupation did Joseph, Jesus' earthly father, practice?

3. Match: Demetrius. . .
   a) silversmith in Ephesus
   b) helper of Paul in Macedonia
   c) spokesman for Jews in Ephesus

4. What disciple was martyred by an angry, screaming crowd after a critical speech to the Sanhedrin?

5. Paul said he was Jewish so the Roman Christians would know that
   a) God has not forgotten His chosen people.
   b) Paul was better than the Roman Christians.
   c) Paul had paid handsomely to have a professional trace his family line.
   d) Paul was eligible to be a member of Boy Scouts.

ANSWERS

1. Paul the Apostle
2. carpentry (Matthew 13:53–55)
3. a (Acts 19:24, 26)
4. Stephen (Acts 7:51–60)
5. a (Romans 11:1–2)

Day 83

1. What was the two-letter name of Job's homeland?

2. Connect the Thoughts:
   Fair Havens
   Syracuse
   Three Taverns

3. When Moses fled from Egypt, to what country did he go?

4. Match: Pool of Siloam. . .
   a) where Jesus sent a blind man
   b) where Jesus sent a demon-possessed man
   c) where Jesus sent a woman who was bleeding

5. What tribe of Israel, which could not occupy its allotted place in the Promised Land, took over somewhere else?

ANSWERS

1. Uz (Job 1:1)
2. stops on Paul's journey to Rome (Acts 27:1–8; Acts 28:12–14; Acts 28:14–15)
3. Midian (Exodus 2:15)
4. a (John 9:1–7)
5. Dan (Judges 18)

Day 84

1. On the Sabbath, Jesus healed a man stricken with
   a) a withered hand.
   b) blindness.
   c) deafness.
   d) paralysis.

2. What three-word phrase did the resurrected Jesus repeat while reinstating Peter?

3. Match: Jesus. . .
   a) made no promises about the Holy Spirit.
   b) promised eternal life if we believe in Him.
   c) promised His coming would bring peace to families.

4. What great king of Israel did Jesus once quote from the book of Psalms?

5. Complete the scripture:
   Looking unto Jesus the ____ and finisher of our faith. . .

ANSWERS

1. a (Matthew 12:6–13; Mark 3:1–5; Luke 6:6–10)
2. "Feed my sheep" (John 21:15–19 KJV).
3. b (John 3:16)
4. David (Luke 20:39–44)
5. author (Hebrews 12:2 KJV)

Day 85

1. What weapon did David use to knock down the giant Goliath?
    a) a machine gun
    b) a bow and arrow
    c) a spear
    d) a sling

2. What moldable material, according to Jeremiah, represented Israel in the hands of God?

3. Isaiah prophesied of a time when the nations would beat their swords into what?
    a) plowshares
    b) anvils
    c) goblets
    d) the ground

4. What was the purpose for the three pairs of wings on the seraphims?

5. According to David, God's spiritual cleansing makes us whiter than what?
    a) dried bones
    b) snow
    c) clouds
    d) wool

ANSWERS

1. d (1 Samuel 17:49–50)
2. clay (Jeremiah 18:1–6)
3. a (Isaiah 2:4)
4. one set to cover their faces, one set to cover their feet, and one set to fly with (Isaiah 6:2)
5. b (Psalm 51:7)

Day 86

1. What three words complete God's promise, "It is mine to avenge," quoted by Paul in his letter to the Romans?

2. Connect the Thoughts:
    saying, "There is no God"
    despising a father's instruction
    trusting in one's self

3. True or False: Idolatry is the worship of false gods.

4. When Cain went out of the Lord's presence, he went to live in
    a) Mod.
    b) Nod.
    c) Sod.
    d) Cod.

5. What sin did the apostle Paul tell the Thessalonians is likely to occur at night?

ANSWERS

1. "I will repay" (Romans 12:19 NIV).
2. things relating to fools (Psalm 14:1; Proverbs 15:5; Proverbs 28:26)
3. True
4. b (Genesis 4:16)
5. drunkenness (1 Thessalonians 5:7)

Day 87

1. What, according to Jesus, would set free the crowds who followed Him?

2. What does the apostle Paul, in the book of Romans, say Christians are *not* under, now that they are under grace?
   a) condemnation
   b) the flesh
   c) the law
   d) the curse

3. Complete this sentence:
   Jesus said that "with God all things are ____."

4. What *S* word, meaning "to yield," does James urge Christians to do to God?

5. Match: Parable of two men who prayed. . .
   a) The tax collector fasted once a week.
   b) The Pharisee fasted twice a week.
   c) The tax collector fasted twice a week.

ANSWERS

1. the truth (John 8:31–32)
2. c (Romans 6:14–15)
3. possible (Matthew 19:26)
4. submit (James 4:7)
5. b (Luke 18:9–13)

Day 88

1. How many demons were cast out of Mary Magdalene?

2. Connect the Thoughts:
    shepherd
    green pastures
    a table "in the presence of mine enemies"

3. What five books of the Bible did Moses write?

4. Match: Malachi. . .
    a) After him, no prophet would speak God's voice for five hundred years.
    b) He wrote of the prophet Elijah's return.
    c) He wrote encouraging the rebuilding of the temple.

5. Why did Saul want to be soothed by music?

ANSWERS

1. seven (Luke 8:2)
2. Psalm 23 KJV
3. the Pentateuch—Genesis, Exodus, Leviticus, Numbers, Deuteronomy
4. b (Malachi 4:5)
5. because God had sent an evil spirit to bother rebellious Saul (1 Samuel 16:15–17)

Day 89

1. Connect the Thoughts:
   the Jordan River
   "Thou art my beloved Son."
   John the Baptist

2. What four things did Jesus say "thou shalt love the Lord thy God with all thy"?

3. Complete the scripture:
   Who is he that overcometh the world, but he that believeth that Jesus is the ___ ___ ___?

4. How did Pilate's wife describe Jesus?

5. Match: Lamb of God. . .
   a) Jesus did not celebrate Passover the year He was crucified.
   b) Only Jesus as the Lamb was worthy to open the seven seals.
   c) Jesus was crucified by Himself.

ANSWERS

1. Jesus' baptism (Mark 1:4, 9–11 KJV)
2. heart, soul, mind, strength (Mark 12:30 KJV)
3. Son of God (1 John 5:5 KJV)
4. a just or innocent man (Matthew 27:17–19)
5. b (Revelation 5:5, 8)

Day 90

1. What prophet went through an earthquake only to learn that God spoke in a gentle whisper?

2. When Satan placed boils on him, Job scratched them with
   a) broken pottery.
   b) his fingernails.
   c) the dull edge of a knife.
   d) the tip of a stick.

3. True or False: Rebekah gave Jacob the idea that he should deceive his father to steal Esau's blessing.

4. What wayward prophet actually complained that God is "a gracious God, and merciful, slow to anger, and of great kindness"?

5. Connect the Thoughts:
   son of Nun
   successor of Moses
   leader of Israel

ANSWERS

1. Elijah (1 Kings 19:11–13)
2. a (Job 2:7–8 NIV)
3. True (Genesis 27:6–10)
4. Jonah (Jonah 4:1–2 KJV)
5. Joshua (Numbers 27:18–20)

Day 91

1. What miraculous sign, interpreted by Daniel, foretold the doom of King Belshazzar?

2. Connect the Thoughts:
   Two witnesses are killed and resurrected in Jerusalem.
   Satan is bound for one thousand years.
   God wipes tears from believers' eyes.

3. Match: Crossing the Red Sea. . .
   a) God led the Hebrews through the wilderness to the Red Sea.
   b) Aaron carried the bones of Joseph across the Red Sea.
   c) Aaron stretched out his hand over the Red Sea.

4. True or False: The Feast of Trumpets took place to commemorate the seventh month.

5. What two people had time altered for them?

ANSWERS

1. the handwriting on the wall (Daniel 5)
2. events in the book of Revelation (Revelation 11:3–12; Revelation 20:1–2; Revelation 21:3–4)
3. a (Exodus 13:18)
4. True (Leviticus 23:23–24)
5. Joshua, Hezekiah (Joshua 10:13; 2 Kings 20:8–11)

Day 92

1. What was the first immediate effect on Jesus' disciples upon receiving the Holy Spirit?

2. No one will see God without
   a) a certificate of baptism.
   b) permission from Saint Peter at the pearly gates.
   c) teaching Sunday School for twenty years.
   d) holiness.

3. Whom will you love if you also love God?

4. True or False: In Old Testament times, people never prayed directly to God.

5. Jesus says that God
   a) shows mercy only to those who love Him.
   b) remembers only those who thank Him for His goodness.
   c) is kind to everyone, including the evil and unthankful.
   d) will destroy our enemies if we ask Him.

ANSWERS

1. They began to speak in different languages (tongues) (Acts 1:13, 2:4).
2. d (Hebrews 12:14)
3. People who love God love their brother (1 John 4:21).
4. False (Genesis 24:12, 25:21; 1 Samuel 8:6; and many more!)
5. c (Luke 6:35)

Day 93

1. Match: Paul, in Jerusalem. . .
   a) was transferred directly from there to Rome.
   b) was told by his nephew of a plot to kill him.
   c) preached at the site of an idol to an unknown god.

2. What missionary companion of Paul experienced an earthquake in a Philippian jail?

3. True or False: Because he was taken to Felix, Paul was rescued from certain death at the hands of more than forty Jews who opposed his teachings.

4. Whom did Paul say tried to keep him from making progress?

5. Gaius was
   a) a strong Christian who walked in the truth.
   b) a pagan John was trying to convert.
   c) one of the twelve disciples.
   d) a rich merchant who gave John millions of dollars to run his ministry.

ANSWERS

1. b (Acts 23:14, 16)
2. Silas (Acts 16:25–26)
3. True (Acts 23:12–24)
4. Satan (1 Thessalonians 2:18)
5. a (3 John 1–3)

Day 94

1. Match: Valley of Elah. . .
    a) where Saul's army camped to meet Goliath
    b) where Solomon was made king
    c) where Satan tempted Jesus

2. What terrible locale, according to Jesus, is a place where "the fire is not quenched"?

3. Connect the Thoughts:
    Zin
    Paran
    Sinai

4. Where were the two disciples headed when Jesus walked with them after His resurrection?

5. What place did the Lord name that means "Is the Lord among us or not?"

ANSWERS

1. a (1 Samuel 17:2–4)
2. hell (Mark 9:45–48)
3. wildernesses, or deserts (Numbers 33:36; Genesis 21:21; Exodus 19:1)
4. Emmaus (Luke 24:12–15)
5. Meribah (Exodus 17:7)

Day 95

1. Connect the Thoughts:
   the pure in heart
   the merciful
   they that mourn

2. How did Jesus describe the yoke He places on His followers?

3. Complete the scripture:
   As the Father hath loved me, so have I loved you: ____ ye in my love.

4. Who described Jesus as the "Lamb of God, who takes away the sin of the world"?

5. The adulteress' accusers interrupted Jesus as He was
   a) eating.
   b) praying.
   c) teaching.
   d) sleeping.

ANSWERS

1. people Jesus blessed in His Beatitudes (Matthew 5:1–10)
2. easy (Matthew 11:28–30)
3. continue (John 15:9 KJV)
4. John the Baptist (John 1:29 NIV)
5. c (John 8:2–4)

Day 96

1. What kind of animals rushed into a lake and drowned after receiving demons cast from humans?

2. Peter saw a vision that showed him it is permissible to
   a) eat food that had been sacrificed to idols.
   b) eat only animals considered clean under Jewish law.
   c) be a vegetarian.
   d) eat all sorts and kinds of animals.

3. What creatures did Jesus cite as having homes when "the Son of Man has no place to lay his head"?

4. Connect the Thoughts:
   the seven spirits of God before His throne
   "Thy word"
   five wise and five foolish virgins

5. What plague in Egypt came first, the frogs or the lice?

ANSWERS

1. pigs (Matthew 8:28–32)
2. d (Acts 10:9–18)
3. foxes and birds (Luke 9:58 NIV)
4. lamps (Revelation 4:5; Psalm 119:105 KJV; Matthew 25:1–13)
5. frogs (Exodus 8:5–17)

Day 97

1. What extreme advice did Jesus have for a person whose "right hand offend thee"—indicating the seriousness of dealing with sin?

2. Jude was upset with ungodly men in the church because they
   a) did not give their full 10 percent tithe.
   b) denied the Lord God and His Son Jesus Christ.
   c) sacrificed bulls instead of bullocks.
   d) spent all of the church's money on themselves.

3. What, according to James, is the source of every man's temptation?

4. Complete the scripture:
   And when the mourning was past, David sent and fetched her to his house, and she became his wife, and bare him a son. But the thing that David had done ____ the LORD.

5. Moneychangers were in the temple to
   a) provide correct change.
   b) exchange one form of money for another.
   c) drum up support.
   d) take bets on races in the Coliseum.

ANSWERS

1. cut it off (Matthew 5:30 KJV)
2. b (Jude 1:4)
3. his own lust, or evil desire (James 1:14)
4. displeased (2 Samuel 11:27 KJV)
5. b (John 2:13–16)

Day 98

1. According to the Proverbs, a good wife wears
    a) plenty of red lipstick.
    b) the crown of life.
    c) joy unspeakable.
    d) strength and honor.

2. What type of person did Jesus use to contrast with the self-righteous Pharisees in a parable on humility?

3. Complete the scripture:
    For as the body without the spirit is ___, so faith without works is ___ also.

4. When someone wrongs you, what does Jesus say you should do first?

5. What was the apostle Peter's command regarding grace?
    a) remember
    b) share
    c) grow in
    d) pursue

ANSWERS

1. d (Proverbs 31:10, 25)
2. a tax collector, or publican (Luke 18:9–14)
3. dead, dead (James 2:26 KJV)
4. Go and show him his fault, between the two of you (Matthew 18:15).
5. c (2 Peter 3:18)

Day 99

1. Match: Amos. . .
    a) was shown a plumbline by God.
    b) was shown a bowl of spoiled fruit by God.
    c) was the son of a priest.

2. What did the apostle Paul say that long hair is to a woman?

3. Connect the Thoughts:
    bath
    cor
    homer

4. To what kind of weapon does the writer of Hebrews compare the Word of God?

5. The Law in the Pentateuch is often called the Mosaic Law because
    a) God gave the laws to Moses.
    b) all the laws are different, creating a "mosaic" of instructions.
    c) Moses broke the stone tablets and made up his own law.
    d) Moses was a police officer.

ANSWERS

1. a (Amos 7:8)
2. glory (1 Corinthians 11:15)
3. units of liquid measurement (Ezekiel 45:14)
4. double-edged sword (Hebrews 4:12 NIV)
5. a

Day 100

1. What is the Great Commission that Jesus gave His disciples before being taken up to heaven?

2. Jesus healed the Canaanite woman's daughter because
   a) her faith was great.
   b) He wanted to extend His ministry to the Gentiles.
   c) He wanted to show love for enemies.
   d) she washed His feet with perfume.

3. Connect the Thoughts:
   our Father
   our debts
   our daily bread

4. Jesus said, "Heaven and earth will pass away. . ." but what two-word answer would not?

5. A listing of Jesus' ancestors, or His lineage, is found
   a) in Matthew and Luke.
   b) in Mark and John.
   c) in Genesis and Revelation.
   d) in New York's Museum of Modern Art.

ANSWERS

1. "Go into all the world and preach the gospel to all creation" (Mark 16:15, 19 NIV).
2. a (Matthew 15:21–28)
3. the Lord's Prayer (Matthew 6:9–13)
4. "My words" (Matthew 24:35 NIV)
5. a (Matthew 1:1–16; Luke 3:23–38)

Day 101

1. What woman lay at the feet of Boaz in a threshing floor—initiating a relationship that culminated in marriage?

2. True or False: Rachel, Leah, and their handmaids Zilpah and Bilhah were the mothers of the twelve tribes of Israel.

3. Connect the Thoughts:
   younger brother
   murder victim
   keeper of a flock

4. What Old Testament figure chose vegetables—or pulse—and water over his king's meat and wine?
   a) Moses
   b) Daniel
   c) David
   d) Jeremiah

5. Match: Hannah. . .
   a) Her husband, Elkanah, had no children.
   b) Eli the priest thought she was drunk.
   c) Eli's sons told her to leave the temple.

ANSWERS

1. Ruth (Ruth 3:7–9, 4:13)
2. True (Genesis 29:31–30:24, 35:16–18).
3. Abel (Genesis 4:1–8)
4. b (Daniel 1:8–12)
5. b (1 Samuel 1:12–13)

Day 102

1. What transportation disaster befell the apostle Paul as he was traveling to Rome to stand trial before Caesar?

2. Match: Paul's shipwreck. . .
    a) occurred in the Mediterranean Sea.
    b) occurred in the Ionian Sea.
    c) occurred in the Adriatic Sea.

3. How many days did the Feast of Unleavened Bread last?

4. How did the Roman soldiers hasten the deaths of the robbers crucified with Jesus?
    a) by giving them poison
    b) by cutting off their heads
    c) by spearing them
    d) by breaking their legs

5. What bad man got his head nailed to the ground?

ANSWERS

1. shipwreck (Acts 27)
2. c (Acts 27:27, 41 NIV)
3. seven days (Exodus 12:18–19)
4. d (John 19:32)
5. Sisera (Judges 4:2–3, 17, 21)

Day 103

1. How did God show His presence at the dedication of Solomon's temple?

2. Fill in the blank:
Paul writes in 2 Corinthians that we praise a "Father of compassion and the God of all ____."

3. According to the Proverbs, a gentle answer turns away what?
   a) wrath
   b) enemies
   c) arguments
   d) lawsuits

4. True or False: God did not have any special consideration for the poor until Jesus spoke about them in the New Testament.

5. What is the first of God's Ten Commandments?

ANSWERS

1. Fire came down from heaven and consumed the sacrifices; God's glory filled the place (2 Chronicles 6:10, 12, 7:1).
2. comfort (2 Corinthians 1:3 NIV)
3. a (Proverbs 15:1 NIV)
4. False. Many of God's Old Testament laws contained provisions for the poor.
5. "Thou shalt have no other gods before me" (Exodus 20:3 KJV).

Day 104

1. According to Jesus, who will inherit the earth?
    a) the environmentalists
    b) the merciful
    c) the peacemakers
    d) the meek

2. What notorious prisoner gained his freedom from Pontius Pilate as Jesus was sentenced to crucifixion?

3. Connect the Thoughts:
    Amplias
    Nymphas
    Andronicus

4. What nationality, hated by the Jews, provided the "good guy" character in Jesus' parable of a man beaten by robbers?

5. Match: Zechariah. . .
    a) was told by the angel to name his son John.
    b) received the message from the angel Michael.
    c) was visited by the angel at his home in Jerusalem.

ANSWERS

1. d (Matthew 5:5)
2. Barabbas (Matthew 27:24–26)
3. people the apostle Paul greeted in his epistles (Romans 16:8; Colossians 4:15; Romans 16:7)
4. Samaritan (Luke 10:25–37)
5. a (Luke 1:11–20, 39–40)

Day 105

1. What mountain was the setting for Moses' encounter with God in a burning bush?

2. Connect the Thoughts:
   Jabbok
   Ulai
   Kishon

3. Toward the end of his life, Jeremiah was taken captive to what country?

4. Match: The new Jerusalem. . .
   a) has no temple.
   b) has a sun and moon.
   c) has gates that close at night.

5. From what location did Moses send the twelve spies into the Promised Land?

ANSWERS

1. Horeb (Exodus 3:1–6)
2. rivers (Deuteronomy 3:16; Daniel 8:2 KJV; Judges 5:21)
3. Egypt (Jeremiah 43:1–7)
4. a (Revelation 21)
5. wilderness of Paran (Numbers 13:1–17)

Day 106

1. To whom did Jesus first appear following His resurrection?

2. The two sources that trace Jesus' lineage differ from David to Jesus. This is because
   a) neither one is accurate.
   b) the records in Bethlehem burned.
   c) one source had to guess at names after a computer crash.
   d) one traces Joseph's line from David, while the other traces Mary's ancestors.

3. Seated on the throne in the book of Revelation, Jesus tells the disciple John, "I am making everything ____!"

4. Connect the Thoughts:
   the meek
   the poor in spirit
   the peacemakers

5. According to Paul, how was Jesus in the wilderness with Moses and the children of Israel?

ANSWERS

1. Mary Magdalene and another Mary (Matthew 28)
2. d
3. new (Revelation 21:2–5 NIV)
4. people Jesus blessed in His Beatitudes (Matthew 5:1–10)
5. as the spiritual Rock that followed them (1 Corinthians 10:1–4)

Day 107

1. What swarming insects stripped Egypt of every green plant in the eighth plague called down by Moses?

2. Who is known as the "father of all who play the harp"?
   a) David
   b) Jubal
   c) Seth
   d) Asaph

3. To what animals did Jesus liken His disciples and the unbelievers to whom they would be sent?

4. What kind of branches did people spread before Jesus during His "triumphal entry" into Jerusalem?
   a) olive
   b) oak
   c) palm
   d) sycamore

5. To what creature did God say, "I will put enmity between thee and the woman"?

ANSWERS

1. locusts (Exodus 10:13–15)
2. b (Genesis 4:21 NIV)
3. sheep among wolves (Matthew 10:16)
4. c (John 12:12–13)
5. the serpent (Genesis 3:14–15 KJV)

Day 108

1. What two disciples let their anger get the best of them by suggesting that a Samaritan village that had snubbed Jesus be destroyed by fire from heaven?

2. How did Jesus respond to His disciples' comment above?
   a) He wept.
   b) He rebuked them.
   c) He prayed.
   d) He ignored them.

3. What false goddess, called by some "the queen of heaven," was pursued by Solomon?

4. Complete the scripture:
   Your iniquities have separated between you and your God, and your sins have hid his face from you, that he will not ___.

5. Why were the children of Israel condemned to wander in the wilderness for forty years?

ANSWERS

1. James and John (Luke 9:50–54)
2. b (Luke 9:55–56)
3. Ashtoreth (1 Kings 11:5)
4. hear (Isaiah 59:2 KJV)
5. because they refused to conquer the Promised Land when God told them (Numbers 14)

Day 109

1. What attitude of giving, according to the apostle Paul, does God love?

2. Complete the scripture:
Grow in grace, and in the ___ of our Lord and Saviour Jesus Christ.

3. Which of Paul's letters includes the famous charge, "Study to shew thyself approved unto God"?

4. Another name for Jesus' Sermon on the Mount is
    a) Beatitudes.
    b) Attitude Adjustments.
    c) Beatniks.
    d) Assertiveness Training.

5. When a good woman speaks, what do her words have?

ANSWERS

1. cheerful (2 Corinthians 9:7)
2. knowledge (2 Peter 3:18 KJV)
3. 2 Timothy (2:15 KJV)
4. a
5. wisdom (Proverbs 31:10, 26)

Day 110

1. A psalter
   a) sprinkles salt.
   b) fights wild animals.
   c) copies manuscripts.
   d) offers praises to God.

2. What son of David cut his long hair whenever it became too heavy for him?

3. Connect the Thoughts:
   the rainfall of Noah's flood
   Jesus' fast in the wilderness
   Jesus' post-resurrection appearances

4. Match: Nahum. . .
   a) predicted Babylon's doom.
   b) predicted Nineveh's destruction.
   c) predicted fifty more prosperous years for Nineveh.

5. What is the last book of the New Testament?

ANSWERS

1. d
2. Absalom (2 Samuel 3:2–3, 14:25–26)
3. forty days (Genesis 7:11–12; Luke 4:1–2; Acts 1:1–3)
4. b (Nahum 1:8, 14)
5. Revelation

Day 111

1. Complete the scripture:
   Then said Jesus, Father, ____ them; for they know not what they do.

2. On two occasions, Jesus is recorded as feeding crowds numbering in the thousands. How many were in each crowd?

3. What did Jesus say would not prevail against His church?
   a) the sins of mankind
   b) the armies of Satan
   c) the gates of Hades
   d) the forces of evil

4. What *S* word completes Jesus' sentence: "I desire mercy, not ____."

5. True or False: Jesus doubted the sincerity of Zacchaeus' repentance.

ANSWERS

1. forgive (Luke 23:34 KJV)
2. Five thousand men, plus women and children; and four thousand men, plus women and children (Matthew 14:13–21, 15:32–38)
3. c (Matthew 16:17–18)
4. sacrifice (Matthew 12:7 NIV)
5. False (Luke 19:8–9)

Day 112

1. What woman was Jacob tricked into marrying by his devious uncle Laban?

2. Connect the Thoughts:
   King Eglon of Moab
   King Joash of Judah
   King Sennacherib of Assyria

3. Who were Miriam's brothers?

4. Complete the scripture:
   ____ came I out of my mother's womb, and ____ shall I return thither: the LORD gave, and the LORD hath taken away; blessed be the name of the LORD."

5. Hagar was
   a) a handmaid.
   b) an Egyptian.
   c) the mother of Ishmael as a result of Sarah's decision.
   d) all of the above.

ANSWERS

1. Leah (Genesis 29:13, 21–25)
2. victims of assassination (Judges 3:12–25; 2 Kings 12:19–20; 2 Kings 19:36–37)
3. Aaron and Moses (1 Chronicles 6:3)
4. naked, naked (Job 1:21 KJV)
5. d (Genesis 16:1, 3–11)

Day 113

1. The Feast of Unleavened Bread began
   a) the day after Passover.
   b) the day before Passover.
   c) on Moses' birthday.
   d) when everyone ran out of yeast.

2. Which day of creation included God making night?

3. Connect the Thoughts:
   the feeding of five thousand
   the healing of Jairus' daughter
   an unexpected catch of fish

4. What did Heber's wife, Jael, do that made her famous?

5. Match: The Flood. . .
   a) Noah was five hundred years old when the Flood came.
   b) Noah took seven pairs of every clean animal onto the ark.
   c) The waters flooded the earth for fifty days.

ANSWERS

1. a (Numbers 28:16–17)
2. the first (Genesis 1:5)
3. miracles of Jesus (Matthew 14:13–21; Mark 5:22–42; Luke 5:1–6)
4. She nailed a man's head to the ground (Judges 4:21).
5. b (Genesis 7:1–2, 5)

Day 114

1. What is the Aramaic word for "father" or "daddy"?

2. To show us His love, God
   a) sent His only begotten Son into the world, that we might live through Him.
   b) sent manna to all Christians.
   c) promised vast wealth to all Christians.
   d) promised that one day we would have pictures of Mars.

3. Who has not seen God?

4. True or False: The "Father's house" is another way of saying heaven.

5. What name for Himself does God say He used when appearing to Abraham, Isaac, and Jacob?

ANSWERS

1. Abba (Romans 8:15)
2. a (1 John 4:9)
3. people who do evil (3 John 11)
4. True (John 14:2)
5. God Almighty (Exodus 6:3)

Day 115

1. What synagogue official saw his twelve-year-old daughter raised to life by Jesus?

2. True or False: Felix was married to a Jewess named Drusilla.

3. Who asked Jesus to let the sons of Zebedee sit at each side of Jesus in His kingdom?

4. Connect the Thoughts:
   Jesus in Samaria
   a request for a drink
   five husbands

5. Match: Joseph, husband of Mary. . .
   a) He was not a direct descendant of David.
   b) The seer Simeon told him to flee to Egypt with Jesus.
   c) He wanted to obtain a divorce from Mary.

ANSWERS

1. Jairus (Luke 8:41–56)
2. True (Acts 24:24)
3. their mother (Matthew 20:20–21)
4. the woman at the well (John 4:1–26)
5. c (Matthew 1:16–19, 2:13–14; Luke 2:25–35)

Day 116

1. Of the four rivers that were said to flow from the Garden of Eden, what two share names with important rivers of the modern Middle East?

2. Connect the Thoughts:
   Ephesus
   Smyrna
   Thyatira

3. What town was home to Zacchaeus?

4. Match: Gaza. . .
   a) where Samson asked to die with the Philistines
   b) where Samson met his wife
   c) a city of Benjamin

5. Where was Eve in the Garden of Eden when the serpent spoke to her?

ANSWERS

1. Tigris and Euphrates (Genesis 2:10–14)
2. churches of Revelation (Revelation 2:1; Revelation 2:8; Revelation 2:18)
3. Jericho (Luke 19:1–6)
4. a (Judges 16:20–30)
5. in the center (Genesis 2:9, 3:6)

Day 117

1. Daniel refers to Jesus as the "Ancient of ____"?

2. What did certain Jews call Jesus after He proclaimed, "If anyone keeps my word, he will never see death"?

3. True or False: John wrote down everything that Jesus did.

4. What Roman official asked Jesus to heal his servant?
   a) a centurion
   b) a general
   c) a proconsul
   d) a governor

5. Connect the Thoughts:
   James the son of Alphaeus
   Simon the Canaanite
   Thomas

ANSWERS

1. Days (Daniel 7:13 NIV)
2. demon-possessed (John 8:49–52 NIV)
3. False (John 21:25)
4. a (Matthew 8:8)
5. disciples of Jesus (Matthew 10:2–4 KJV)

Day 118

1. What musical instrument did Miriam, Aaron's sister, play?
    a) horn
    b) harp
    c) flute
    d) tambourine

2. What substance did God use to form the first man?

3. Connect the Thoughts:
    Jonah's plant
    Herod's death
    hell's immortal creatures

4. What ravenous animal would feed peacefully with the lamb in the new earth prophesied by Isaiah?

5. What did Paul suggest Timothy should take for his frequent illnesses?
    a) wine
    b) cheese
    c) honey
    d) herbs

ANSWERS

1. d (Exodus 15:20)
2. dust (Genesis 2:7)
3. worms (Jonah 4:6–8; Acts 12:21–23; Mark 9:44–46)
4. wolf (Isaiah 65:18, 25)
5. a (1 Timothy 5:23)

Day 119

1. What king of Assyria insulted God to King Hezekiah of Judah—and paid for it with his life?

2. What did a seraph touch to Isaiah's lips to take away his guilt and sin?
   a) a golden bowl
   b) a budding pole
   c) a live coal
   d) a sealed scroll

3. What false prophet prophesied against Jeremiah and died?

4. When Jonah tried to escape God's will, he
   a) was swallowed by a big fish.
   b) proved successful in his attempt to escape.
   c) told God he would go to Nineveh if He would name a Bible book after him.
   d) wrote a book called *Jonah's Travels*.

5. Complete the scripture:
   If we claim to be without sin, we ____ ourselves and the truth is not in us.

ANSWERS

1. Sennacherib (2 Kings 19:5–13, 35–37)
2. c (Isaiah 6:6–7)
3. Hananiah (Jeremiah 28)
4. a (Jonah 1)
5. deceive (1 John 1:8 NIV)

Day 120

1. What is more important than beauty in a good woman?

2. Jesus said to store your treasures in
   a) the stock market.
   b) other people.
   c) real estate.
   d) heaven.

3. What did the apostle Paul say is profitable, or useful, for teaching, rebuking, correcting, and training in righteousness?

4. Complete the scripture:
   Bear ye one another's burdens, and so ___ the law of Christ.

5. In a parable describing the kingdom of heaven, where did Jesus say a man found a hidden treasure?

ANSWERS

1. fear of the Lord (Proverbs 31:30)
2. d (Matthew 6:20)
3. scripture (2 Timothy 3:16)
4. fulfil (Galatians 6:2 KJV)
5. in a field (Matthew 13:44)

Day 121

1. Match: Zephaniah. . .
    a) wrote during the reign of King Josiah.
    b) was the son of Pethuel.
    c) wrote during the reign of King Uzziah.

2. What Philistine idol fell over and broke in pieces when the ark of the covenant was placed nearby?

3. Connect the Thoughts:
    Naaman at the Jordan River
    Pontius Pilate's hands
    Jesus and the disciples' feet

4. A prophet is
    a) an astronomer.
    b) a psychic.
    c) one who interprets dreams.
    d) one sent by God to tell His plans for the future.

5. How many of Peter's letters are included in the Bible?

ANSWERS

1. a (Zephaniah 1:1)
2. Dagon (1 Samuel 5:1–5)
3. washing (2 Kings 5:11–14; Matthew 27:24; John 13:3–5)
4. d
5. two

Day 122

1. Who did Jesus tell an expert in the law he should love as himself?

2. Complete this scripture from Matthew describing Jesus: I will open my mouth in parables, I will utter things hidden since ____ ____ ____ ____ ____.

3. Like Daniel, in the book of Revelation, John describes Jesus as having hair of what color?

4. Connect the Thoughts:
   a withered hand made well
   a fig tree cursed
   a coin found in a fish's mouth

5. What were Jesus' last words on the cross?

ANSWERS

1. (his) neighbor (Matthew 22:34–39)
2. the creation of the world (Matthew 13:35 NIV, referring to Psalm 78:2)
3. white (as wool and snow) (Revelation 1:13–14)
4. miracles of Jesus (Luke 6:6–10; Matthew 21:18–22; Matthew 17:24–27)
5. "Father, into thy hands I commend my spirit" (Luke 23:46 KJV).

Day 123

1. What nationality of woman did Samson, to his parents' disgust, seek out for a wife?

2. Mephiboseth was
   a) blind.
   b) lame in both feet.
   c) a leper.
   d) deaf.

3. Connect the Thoughts:
   Ahinoam
   Abigail
   Michal

4. Match: Elizabeth. . .
   a) Mary stayed with her for six months.
   b) Her husband regained his sight at their son's birth.
   c) Her husband said their son would be a prophet.

5. Who was Cain and Abel's brother?

ANSWERS

1. Philistine (Judges 14:1–3)
2. b (2 Samuel 9:13)
3. wives of King David (1 Samuel 30:5; 1 Samuel 19:11)
4. c (Luke 1:63, 67, 76)
5. Seth (Genesis 4:25)

Day 124

1. What did scoffers accuse the disciples of when they spoke in tongues at Pentecost?

2. Connect the Thoughts:
   Jesus' ascension into heaven
   the Holy Spirit's arrival at Pentecost
   the deaths of Ananias and Sapphira

3. Match: Siege of Jerusalem. . .
   a) described by Ezekiel in words God gave him
   b) ended by Ezekiel putting on ashes and sackcloth
   c) depicted by a model Ezekiel built

4. How many days did the people celebrate following the completion of Solomon's temple?

5. What annual occasion witnessed the priest using the scapegoat?

ANSWERS

1. drunkenness (Acts 2:1–15)
2. events in the book of Acts (Acts 1:1–11; Acts 2:1–4; Acts 5:1–11)
3. c (Ezekiel 3:24, 4:1–3)
4. fourteen (1 Kings 8:20, 65)
5. Day of Atonement (Leviticus 16)

Day 125

1. What name did Jesus use for the Holy Spirit?

2. Fill in the blank:
   Jesus tells us that in His Father's house are many ____.

3. When we go to God in prayer, we should
   a) be humble.
   b) convince Him how great we are.
   c) give Him a list of our accomplishments in church.
   d) tell Him all about the latest *Star Wars* movie.

4. What name of God, which is *El-Elyon* in Hebrew, was used to describe the God whom the high priest Melchizedek served?

5. Who tried to buy the gifts of the Holy Spirit?

ANSWERS

1. Comforter (KJV), Counselor (NIV) (John 15:26)
2. rooms (NIV) or mansions (KJV) (John 14:2)
3. a (2 Chronicles 7:14)
4. most high God (Genesis 14:18 KJV)
5. Simon the sorcerer (Acts 8:9, 18–19)

Day 126

1. What devout man held the baby Jesus when Mary and Joseph presented Him at the temple?

2. Connect the Thoughts:
   James the son of Zebedee
   Thaddaeus
   Bartholomew

3. The repentant criminal who was crucified with Jesus asked Him to
   a) remember him.
   b) reward him for defending Him against the other criminal.
   c) save him.
   d) be buried with him.

4. Match: Mary, earthly mother of Jesus. . .
   a) She and Joseph offered a pair of goats when they presented Jesus at the temple courts.
   b) She received a blessing from Simeon.
   c) She received a blessing from the young prophetess Anna.

5. Who was the first person killed because he believed in Christ?

ANSWERS

1. Simeon (Luke 2:25–32)
2. disciples of Jesus (Matthew 10:2–4)
3. a (Luke 23:39–42)
4. b (Luke 2:34)
5. Stephen (Acts 7:56–60)

Day 127

1. What lodging place in Bethlehem turned away Joseph and his very expectant wife, Mary?

2. Peter wrote his first letter to the elect in
   a) Pontus and Galatia.
   b) Asia.
   c) Cappadocia and Bithynia.
   d) all of the above.

3. Match: Hebron. . .
   a) where Lot chose to live
   b) where Abimelech and Abraham swore an oath
   c) near the Cave of Machpelah

4. What was the "great city," or capital, of Assyria?

5. What did Jonah do inside the giant fish?
   a) practice karate
   b) pray
   c) cry
   d) build a fire

ANSWERS

1. inn (Luke 2:4–7)
2. d (1 Peter 1:1–2)
3. c (Genesis 23:1–2, 19)
4. Nineveh (Genesis 10:11–12 NIV; Jonah 3:3)
5. b (Jonah 2:1)

Day 128

1. What two *W* words did Jesus' disciples utter when they said, "Who is this? Even the ____ and the ____ obey him"?

2. True or False: The Bible tells us Jesus had an active prayer life.

3. Jesus often prayed
   a) loudly, so all would hear.
   b) alone.
   c) only with His disciples, or else others would learn how to pray
   d) only in church.

4. Complete the scripture:
   "Abba, ____," he said, "everything is ____ for you. Take this cup from me. Yet not what I ___, but what you ___."

5. What troublemaking religious leaders—accusing Jesus of casting out demons by the prince of demons—had their thoughts read by Jesus?

ANSWERS

1. wind, waves (Mark 4:40–41 NIV)
2. True (see Mark 1:35 as one example)
3. b (Luke 5:16)
4. Father, possible, will, will (Mark 14:36 NIV)
5. Pharisees (Matthew 12:22–28)

Day 129

1. What kind of animals helped Samson burn the grain fields of his enemies?
   a) lightning bugs
   b) lions
   c) donkeys
   d) foxes

2. What kind of bird, released from the ark, brought an olive leaf back to Noah?

3. Connect the Thoughts:
   Arcturus (the Bear)
   Orion
   Pleiades

4. What animal were the Israelites not to muzzle as it was treading grain (NIV), or corn (KJV)?

5. What did Peter see inside a sheet, coming down from heaven by its four corners?
   a) animals, reptiles, and birds
   b) gold and silver
   c) people of many countries
   d) Christmas presents

ANSWERS

1. d (Judges 15:3–5)
2. dove (Genesis 8:11)
3. constellations (Job 9:9)
4. ox (Deuteronomy 25:4)
5. a (Acts 10:9–12)

Day 130

1. The Lord told Job's visitors that He was
   a) pleased with them.
   b) willing to prosper them.
   c) angry that they were unsuccessful at teaching Job new skills.
   d) angry about their unfaithfulness to Him.

2. What excuse did Adam give for hiding when he heard God's voice?

3. A true prophet
   a) always has good news.
   b) is not always sent from God.
   c) works for profit.
   d) often is sent to warn God's people to repent of sin.

4. What horrible thing did Athaliah do?

5. Connect the Thoughts:
   scribes and Pharisees
   blind guides
   Chorazin and Bethsaida

ANSWERS

1. d (Job 42:7)
2. afraid, naked (either answer acceptable) (Genesis 3:9–10)
3. d
4. killed her grandchildren so she could be queen (2 Kings 11:1–3 KJV)
5. "woe" pronounced by Jesus (Luke 11:44; Matthew 23:16; Luke 10:13 KJV)

Day 131

1. What will happen to the woman who fears the Lord?

2. What did Jesus say He came to call sinners to?

3. Complete the scripture:
   Trust in the LORD with all thine heart; and ___ not unto thine own understanding.

4. James writes that anyone who listens to the Word and does not do what it says is like a man who does what?

5. Connect the Thoughts:
   the Pharisee and the publican, or tax collector
   the rich man and Lazarus
   the lost sheep

ANSWERS

1. She will be praised (Proverbs 31:30).
2. repentance (Luke 5:31–32)
3. lean (Proverbs 3:5 KJV)
4. looks in a mirror and then forgets what he looks like (James 1:23–24)
5. parables of Jesus (Luke 18:9–14; Luke 16:19–31; Luke 15:3–7)

Day 132

1. True or False: Women judges were common in the Old Testament.

2. What four-word phrase is used often in the book of Isaiah to describe the Lord?

3. Connect the Thoughts:
    a parabolic Pharisee, twice a week
    Queen Esther's Jews, for three days
    Jesus, for forty days

4. What part of the body, according to James, "can no man tame"?

5. Match: Joel. . .
    a) son of Pethuel
    b) son of Tekoa
    c) son of Obadiah

ANSWERS

1. False. Deborah was an exception.
2. Holy One of Israel (see, for example, Isaiah 49:7)
3. people who fasted (Luke 18:9–12; Esther 4:15–16; Matthew 4:1–2)
4. the tongue (James 3:8 KJV)
5. a (Joel 1:1)

Day 133

1. What did the terrified disciples think they were seeing when Jesus walked across the water to their boat?

2. True or False: Every spirit that does not acknowledge Jesus is not from God.

3. When Jesus sent forth His twelve disciples the first time, what did He give them the power and authority to do?

4. Complete the scripture:
"Whoever welcomes this little child in my name welcomes ______________________."

5. Only Matthew records Jesus' encounter with two blind men. What do they call Jesus?

ANSWERS

1. a ghost, or spirit (Matthew 14:22–27)
2. True (1 John 4:3 NIV)
3. power and authority over all demons and to cure diseases (Luke 9:1)
4. me (Luke 9:48 NIV)
5. Son of David (Matthew 9:27)

Day 134

1. What daughter did Reuel, a priest of Midian, give to Moses as his wife?

2. What otherwise faithful man once had an embarrassing episode of drunkenness in his tent?
    a) Moses
    b) Joshua
    c) Joseph
    d) Noah

3. Connect the Thoughts:
    the sons—or descendants—of Anak
    Ishbibenob
    Goliath

4. Match: Hagar. . .
    a) She was Abram's first wife.
    b) She and Sarai were half sisters.
    c) She ran away from Sarai.

5. Abraham and Sarah didn't want their son Isaac to marry any of the local women because they were
    a) Canaanites.
    b) Israelites.
    c) members of the Electric Light Orchestra.
    d) ugly.

ANSWERS

1. Zipporah (Exodus 2:16–21)
2. d (Genesis 9:20–21)
3. giants (Numbers 13:33; 2 Samuel 21:16 KJV; 1 Samuel 17:4)
4. c (Genesis 16:8)
5. a (Genesis 24:1–3)

Day 135

1. How many leprous men came to Jesus requesting a mass healing—for which only one returned to praise God?

2. Connect the Thoughts:
   light
   Heaven
   Earth

3. What Old Testament feast was celebrated every month?

4. Match: The Lord's Supper. . .
   a) Bread represented manna in the wilderness.
   b) Bread represented Jesus' body.
   c) Bread represented the bread of the Presence in the tabernacle.

5. How often did the year of Jubilee occur?

ANSWERS

1. ten (Luke 17:11–19)
2. the first three days of creation (Genesis 1:1–13)
3. Feast of the New Moon (1 Samuel 20:5)
4. b (Mark 14:22)
5. every fifty years (Leviticus 25:10)

Day 136

1. What did Jesus tell the disciples that the Holy Spirit would specifically do?

2. Fill in the blank:
   Only Jesus has seen the ____, since He is from God.

3. The Lord spoke to Zechariah through
   a) visions.
   b) a book.
   c) the Lord's web page.
   d) dreams.

4. After Pentecost, how did the apostles impart the Holy Spirit?

5. According to John, what does the Holy Spirit help us do?

ANSWERS

1. abide with them forever (John 14:15–17)
2. Father (John 6:46)
3. a
4. by the laying on of hands (Acts 8:14–17)
5. test the spirits (1 John 4:1–3)

Day 137

1. John said Demetrius was godly because he
   a) did not like Diotrephes.
   b) praised all of John's epistles.
   c) was a true Christian witness.
   d) gave John fine food and lodging.

2. What forbidden art did a Simon from Samaria practice before he accepted Christ?

3. Connect the Thoughts:
   Didymus
   doubting the Resurrection
   "My Lord and my God"

4. Match: Mary and Martha. . .
   a) Martha met Jesus when He arrived after Lazarus's death.
   b) Mary was known to busy herself with household chores.
   c) Mary preferred to sit with Jesus rather than to help Martha.

5. True or False: Another name for Jesus' mother is Mary Magdalene.

ANSWERS

1. c (3 John 12)
2. sorcery (Acts 8:9–24)
3. the apostle Thomas (John 20:24–28)
4. c (Luke 10:38–40; John 11:1–44)
5. False. Mary Magdalene was one of Jesus' followers (Luke 8:1–2).

Day 138

1. In what town did Elijah bring a widow's son back to life?

2. Connect the Thoughts:
   a post-flood migration
   a confusion of languages
   a tower to heaven

3. From what mountain was Moses given a look into the Promised Land?

4. Match: Valley of Jezreel. . .
   a) where David was anointed by Samuel
   b) where Hannah dedicated Samuel to the Lord
   c) where opposing armies were camped to meet Gideon

5. Where did the valiant men bury Saul's bones?

ANSWERS

1. Zarephath (1 Kings 17:8–22)
2. Babel (Genesis 10:32–11:9)
3. Mount Nebo (Deuteronomy 32:48–49)
4. c (Judges 6:33–35)
5. under a tree at Jabesh (1 Samuel 31:12–13)

Day 139

1. When Jesus cried on the cross, "My God, my God, why have you forsaken me?" He was repeating a line from what Old Testament book?

2. Connect the Thoughts:
   Son of Man
   Son of David
   Son of God

3. What famous half-brother could a certain Simon, with his full brothers James, Joseph, and Judas, claim?

4. Complete this scripture spoken by Jesus of the Samaritan who was a good neighbor:
   "Go and do ____."

5. How did Jesus at age twelve refer to the temple in Jerusalem?

ANSWERS

1. the Psalms (see Psalm 22:1 NIV)
2. titles of Jesus Christ (Matthew 8:20; Matthew 1:1; Matthew 8:29–31)
3. Jesus (Matthew 13:53–56)
4. likewise (Luke 10:33, 37 NIV)
5. as His Father's house (Luke 2:49 NIV)

Day 140

1. What judge of Israel had thirty sons who rode thirty donkeys?
   a) Tola
   b) Jair
   c) Jephthah
   d) Eli

2. What color-changing lizard was not permitted on Israelite menus?

3. Connect the Thoughts:
   a cloke (cloak)
   books
   parchments

4. What noisemakers hung off the hem of the priest's garment?

5. Match: Ravens. . .
   a) fed Elisha by the Jordan River.
   b) fed Noah on Mount Ararat.
   c) fed Elijah by the Kerith Ravine.

ANSWERS

1. b (Judges 10:3–4)
2. chameleon (Leviticus 11:29–30)
3. things the apostle Paul wanted in prison (2 Timothy 4:13)
4. bells (Exodus 28:3, 33–34)
5. c (1 Kings 17:2–4)

Day 141

1. An angry man
    a) is a victim of his surroundings.
    b) should be put on the welfare rolls.
    c) stirs up even more anger.
    d) should be allowed to get away with anything he wants.

2. What forbidden tree in the Garden of Eden did the serpent convince Eve to eat from?

3. What disguise does Satan use to try to fool Christians?
    a) a passionate preacher
    b) a wounded traveler
    c) an angel of light
    d) an innocent child

4. Who was cursed with pain in childbirth?

5. A person who will not listen to wise advice will find
    a) poverty and shame.
    b) health and wealth.
    c) his own wisdom.
    d) a new job.

ANSWERS

1. c (Proverbs 29:22)
2. the tree of the knowledge of good and evil (Genesis 2:15–17, 3:1–6)
3. c (2 Corinthians 11:14)
4. Eve (Genesis 3:16–20)
5. a (Proverbs 13:18)

Day 142

1. Which day of the week did the apostle Paul tell believers to put aside money for their offerings?

2. Connect the Thoughts:
   your parents
   better than sacrifice
   God rather than men

3. In Jesus' illustration, what does the man do who loses one sheep out of one hundred?

4. As to our gifts from God, Paul said
   a) all Christians have equal gifts.
   b) we should go to classes to develop our gifts.
   c) that for a small fee, he would help the Romans find their gifts.
   d) we should use whatever gifts God gave us.

5. What is the popular name for Jesus' command to do unto others as you would have them do unto you?

ANSWERS

1. the first day (1 Corinthians 16:1–2)
2. obey (Ephesians 6:1; 1 Samuel 15:22; Acts 5:29)
3. leaves the ninety-nine other sheep and goes to look for that one (Matthew 18:1, 12)
4. d (Romans 12:3–8)
5. the Golden Rule (see Matthew 7:12)

Day 143

1. True or False: In Deborah's time, Israel was a free nation.

2. What body fluid was part of the curse that came by Adam and Eve's sin?

3. Connect the Thoughts:
   Paul
   Achan
   Stephen

4. What kind of lion does the apostle Peter compare the devil to?

5. Match: Fourteen. . .
   a) years Samson was judge of Israel
   b) number of original children of Job
   c) generations from Abraham to David

ANSWERS

1. False (Judges 4:1–4)
2. sweat (Genesis 3:19)
3. people who were stoned (Acts 14:19; Joshua 7:24–26; Acts 7:59)
4. roaring (1 Peter 5:8)
5. c (Matthew 1:17)

Day 144

1. What civic duty did the chief priests and scribes hope to use to get Jesus in trouble with Caesar?

2. Connect the Thoughts:
   "Hosanna!"
   "Hail, King of the Jews!"
   "Crucify him!"

3. To whom did Jesus say, "I tell you the truth, today you will be with me in paradise"?

4. What event did Jesus use as an example to emphasize the need for repentance?
   a) an earthquake in Jerusalem
   b) a tower collapse that killed eighteen people
   c) an outbreak of the plague
   d) the drowning of seven people in a boat accident

5. What name for Jesus, meaning "Anointed One," did the angel of the Lord use when speaking to the shepherds?

ANSWERS

1. paying taxes (Luke 20:19–26)
2. things people shouted at Jesus (John 12:12–13; Matthew 27:27–29; Luke 23:21)
3. one of the criminals crucified with Him (Luke 23:39–43 NIV)
4. b (Luke 13:2–5)
5. Christ (Luke 2:8–11)

Day 145

1. What intelligent and beautiful woman, the wife of the surly Nabal, married King David after Nabal died?

2. What did David take from an unsuspecting King Saul, rather than killing him as David's men urged?
   a) a lock of his hair
   b) a corner of his robe
   c) an arrow from his quiver
   d) a strap from his sandal

3. What term describes Samson, who was never to cut his hair?

4. Connect the Thoughts:
   a drinking party
   handwriting on a wall
   knocking knees

5. Match: Joseph. . .
   a) He dreamed of a vine with three branches that budded.
   b) He wore his coat of many colors in Pharaoh's palace.
   c) He dreamed his brothers bowed down to him.

ANSWERS

1. Abigail (1 Samuel 25:3, 39–42)
2. b (1 Samuel 24:1–11)
3. Nazirite (Judges 13)
4. King Belshazzar (Daniel 5:1–6)
5. c (Genesis 37:5, 9–10)

Day 146

1. How quickly will the glorification of the saints, announced by "the last trumpet," take place?
   a) in the twinkling of an eye
   b) as a horse gallops
   c) in a heartbeat
   d) as the eagle swoops

2. Connect the Thoughts:
   using spit to heal a blind man
   raising Lazarus to life
   walking on water

3. What was the name of the angel who told Mary she would give birth to Jesus?
   a) Michael
   b) Zadok
   c) Gabriel
   d) Hananiah

4. Match: First Passover. . .
   a) raisin cakes
   b) barley bread
   c) bread without yeast

5. Which one of Joseph's brothers kept his other brothers from killing Joseph?
   a) Judah
   b) Benjamin
   c) Dan
   d) Reuben

ANSWERS

1. a (1 Corinthians 15:51–52 NIV)
2. miracles of Jesus (Mark 8:22–25; John 11:38–44; Mark 6:45-50)
3. c (Luke 1:26–31)
4. c (Exodus 12:8, 11)
5. d (Genesis 37:17–21)

Day 147

1. Around whom does the angel of the Lord encamp?

2. Complete this scripture from the book of Hebrews:
   For every house is built by someone, but God is the builder of ____.

3. How did the Holy Spirit empower Moses' seventy elders?

4. According to James, what should a tempted person never say?
   a) "The devil made me do it."
   b) "My own strength shall save me."
   c) "It is of little account."
   d) "God is tempting me."

5. According to Zephaniah 3:17, how does God feel about His people?

ANSWERS

1. all those who fear the Lord (Psalm 34:7)
2. everything (Hebrews 3:4 NIV)
3. they prophesied (Numbers 11:24–25)
4. d (James 1:13)
5. He rejoices over us with singing.

Day 148

1. The Bible tells of a Pharisee who prayed
   a) loudly, boasting about his goodness.
   b) silently.
   c) in French, a language unheard of at that time.
   d) for God to have mercy upon him.

2. Which apostle defended himself before a king named Agrippa—and tried to convert him in the process?

3. True or False: The crowds were pleased by the prospect of Jesus dining with Zacchaeus.

4. Match: Paul. . .
   a) An angel told him he would not stand trial in Rome.
   b) An angel told him only two lives would be lost in a shipwreck.
   c) An angel told him all on board ship would be saved.

5. What religious and political entity, whose name means "sitting together," tried to find false evidence against Jesus?

ANSWERS

1. a (Luke 18:11)
2. Paul (Acts 25:13–26:28)
3. False (Luke 19:5–7)
4. c (Acts 27:23–24)
5. Sanhedrin (Matthew 26:59 NIV)

Day 149

1. When Moses died, in what land did God bury him?

2. What river divided when the prophet Elisha struck it with Elijah's cloak?

3. Connect the Thoughts:
   Tarshish
   Joppa
   Nineveh

4. In what town did Jesus encounter a widow who had lost her only son?

5. What was the potter's field also known as?

ANSWERS

1. in the land of Moab (Deuteronomy 34:5–6)
2. the Jordan (2 Kings 2:12–14)
3. cities in the story of Jonah (Jonah 1:1–3)
4. a town called Nain (Luke 7:11–16)
5. the Field of Blood (Matthew 27:7–8)

Day 150

1. Which of the following sounds will not accompany Jesus' Second Coming?
   a) the trumpet of God
   b) mighty hoof beats
   c) the voice of the archangel
   d) a loud command

2. The shortest verse in the Bible, "Jesus wept," occurs during the telling of what story?

3. Complete the scripture:
   For the Son of man is come to seek and to save that which was ____.

4. Did Jesus know He was to be crucified?

5. Complete Jesus' statement about human souls:
   "The harvest is plentiful. . ."
   a) "and the time is short."
   b) "but the workers are few."
   c) "for the Lord has blessed."
   d) "with the choicest of fruit."

ANSWERS

1. b (1 Thessalonians 4:16 NIV)
2. the raising of Lazarus from the dead (John 11:35 NIV)
3. lost (Luke 19:10 KJV)
4. yes (Matthew 20:17–19)
5. b (Matthew 9:37 NIV)

Day 151

1. What soaring bird, mentioned in Isaiah 40, led Moses' list of flying creatures that could not be eaten?

2. Connect the Thoughts:
   cucumbers
   melons
   leeks

3. How many swords did the disciples take with them when they followed Jesus to the Garden of Gethsemane?

4. Match: Manna. . .
   a) stopped the day after the Israelites ate the bread of Canaan.
   b) tasted like quail.
   c) continued until the Israelites conquered Jericho.

5. Who will judge the angels?

ANSWERS

1. eagle (Leviticus 11:13–19)
2. foods of Egypt, eaten by Israelite slaves (Numbers 11:5)
3. two (Luke 22:38–39)
4. a (Joshua 5:11–12 NIV)
5. Christians (1 Corinthians 6:3)

Day 152

1. What sin of David led to a plague that killed seventy thousand Israelites?
   a) his adultery with Bathsheba
   b) the murder of Uriah
   c) counting the Israelites
   d) polygamy

2. What *W* word does Paul use in Romans 7 to describe himself when torn between doing good and evil?

3. Connect the Thoughts:
   You'll be proven a liar.
   You'll receive plagues.
   You'll lose your part in the book of life.

4. What two descriptions of Satan appear in Revelation 12:9?

5. How did Samuel know that Saul had disobeyed God by failing to completely annihilate the Amalekites?
   a) Saul's shifty eyes
   b) the sound of livestock
   c) Amalekite military stragglers
   d) the Urim and Thummim

ANSWERS

1. c (1 Chronicles 21:1–14)
2. wretched (Romans 7:24 KJV)
3. consequences of manipulating God's Word (Proverbs 30:6; Revelation 22:18; Revelation 22:19)
4. the great dragon, that old serpent (KJV)
5. b (1 Samuel 15:13–19)

Day 153

1. Paul said never to seem
   a) evil.
   b) too friendly to the pagans.
   c) unwilling to share.
   d) uncool.

2. What did the apostle Paul warn the Thessalonians against quenching—or putting out its fire?

3. Connect the Thoughts:
   the fourth commandment
   the seventh day
   rest

4. What two *L* words complete this scripture from Psalms?
   Your word is a ____ to my feet and a ____ for my path.

5. Evil is to be overcome by
   a) evil.
   b) cutting others down.
   c) the sword.
   d) good.

ANSWERS

1. a (1 Thessalonians 5:22)
2. the Spirit (1 Thessalonians 5:19)
3. the Sabbath (Exodus 20:3–11)
4. lamp, light (Psalm 119:105 NIV)
5. d (Romans 12:21)

Day 154

1. What kind of plants and trees did God tell Adam and Eve they could use for food?

2. Complete the scripture:
   I am not ashamed of the gospel of Christ: for it is the ___ of God unto salvation to every one that believeth.

3. What, according to the Song of Solomon, cannot quench love?

4. Connect the Thoughts:
   Paul, at Cenchrea
   Absalom, when it became too heavy
   Samson, by way of Delilah

5. Match: Mandrake plants. . .
   a) Jacob's favorite food
   b) what Leah gave Rachel in return for Jacob
   c) used to make unleavened bread

ANSWERS

1. seed-bearing (Genesis 1:27–29)
2. power (Romans 1:16 KJV)
3. many waters (Song of Solomon 8:7)
4. cutting hair (Acts 18:18; 2 Samuel 14:25–26; Judges 16:18–19)
5. b (Genesis 30:15–16)

Day 155

1. What name did Jesus give to Simon Peter?
   a) Apollos
   b) Cephas
   c) Demas
   d) Festus

2. Who said the following of Jesus? "This child is destined to cause the falling and rising of many in Israel."

3. Connect the Thoughts:
   a man journeying to a far country
   five, two, and one
   "Well done, thou good and faithful servant."

4. Jesus said, "I am the good" what?
   a) beekeeper
   b) shepherd
   c) fisherman
   d) camel driver

5. *Jesus* is the Greek form of what Hebrew name that means "the Lord saves"?

ANSWERS

1. b (John 1:42)
2. Simeon, upon seeing Jesus as a baby (Luke 2:34 NIV)
3. Jesus' parable of the talents (Matthew 25:14–30 KJV)
4. b (John 10:14)
5. Joshua

Day 156

1. What Israelite, as a powerful official in Egypt, forgave his brothers who years before had sold him into slavery?

2. Whose foolish advice, "Curse God and die," did the righteous, suffering Job resist?
    a) Bildad's
    b) Eliphaz's
    c) Zophar's
    d) his wife's

3. What Old Testament prophet healed the waters of Jericho by throwing salt into a spring?

4. Connect the Thoughts:
    Evil-Merodach
    Cyrus
    Nebuchadnezzar

5. Match: Terah. . .
    a) He was the grandfather of Lot.
    b) He was the grandfather of Haran.
    c) He was the grandfather of Nahor.

ANSWERS

1. Joseph (Genesis 50:15–21)
2. d (Job 2:9–10 NIV)
3. Elisha (2 Kings 2:18–22)
4. kings of Babylon (2 Kings 25:27 KJV; Ezra 5:13; 2 Chronicles 36:6)
5. a (Genesis 11:31)

Day 157

1. The stone on the door of Jesus' tomb was rolled back by
    a) Judas.
    b) Mary Magdalene.
    c) Pharaoh.
    d) an angel.

2. True or False: When Goliath challenged the Israelites to send a man to fight him, many men eagerly volunteered.

3. According to the Proverbs, what is worthless "in the day of wrath"?
    a) power
    b) wealth
    c) fame
    d) idols

4. Connect the Thoughts:
    the serpent of Revelation
    the wise and foolish builders
    Noah

5. Match: Jesus' resurrection and defeat of Satan. . .
    a) promised first in Genesis
    b) promised first in Exodus
    c) promised first in Psalms

ANSWERS

1. d (Matthew 28:2–5)
2. False (1 Samuel 17:8–11)
3. b (Proverbs 11:4 NIV)
4. floods (Revelation 12:15–16; Luke 6:47–49; Genesis 7:6)
5. a (Genesis 3:15)

Day 158

1. What name did God give His Son that "is above every name," according to Paul?

2. According to Micah, where does God place forgiven sins?
   a) beyond the stars
   b) the pit of hell
   c) the depths of the sea
   d) gloomy dungeons

3. What does 1 Corinthians 2:12 say that the Holy Spirit is not the spirit of?

4. True or False: God said that some of Abraham's descendants would be kings.

5. What does God mean when He says not to take His name "in vain"?

ANSWERS

1. Jesus (Philippians 2:9–10)
2. c (Micah 7:19)
3. the world
4. True (Genesis 17:1–6)
5. God means we are not to call His name unless we are praying to Him or worshiping Him.

Day 159

1. What job was held by a Simon from Joppa, who entertained the apostle Peter in his house by the sea?

2. What disciple of Jesus apparently had to overcome a negative disposition—as expressed at the death of Lazarus and the resurrection of Christ?
   a) Matthew
   b) Thomas
   c) Bartholomew
   d) Andrew

3. What new father made this statement: "He has raised up a horn of salvation for us in the house of his servant David"?

4. Connect the Thoughts:
   the village of Bethany
   sickness and death
   resurrection

5. What did the name "Barnabas" mean?

ANSWERS

1. tanner (Acts 10:32–33)
2. b (John 11:14–16, 20:24–25)
3. Zechariah, father of John the Baptist (Luke 1:59–60, 67–69 NIV)
4. Lazarus (John 11:1–44)
5. Son of encouragement (Acts 4:36 NIV)

Day 160

1. What city was the birthplace of the apostle Paul?

2. Match: Bethany. . .
   a) where Jesus ascended to heaven
   b) where Jesus fed the five thousand
   c) where Jesus told His disciples to find a donkey tied there

3. In what city was a paralyzed man lowered through a roof to see Jesus?

4. What more familiar name now applies to the ancient city of Jebus?

5. According to the writer of the book of Acts, how far was it from the Mount of Olives to Jerusalem?

ANSWERS

1. Tarsus (Acts 22:2–3)
2. a (Luke 24:50–51)
3. Capernaum (Mark 2:1–5)
4. Jerusalem (Judges 19:10)
5. a Sabbath day's journey (Acts 1:12)

Day 161

1. What two words complete Jesus' statement "I am the bread. . ."?

2. Connect the Thoughts:
    King of the Jews
    the house and lineage of David
    swaddling clothes

3. Filled with compassion, Jesus performs what miracle during the funeral procession for the widow's son?

4. What is Jesus' last statement in the Bible?
    a) "Continue in my love."
    b) "Remember the Lord your God."
    c) "I am coming soon."
    d) "My Father's house awaits you."

5. What two groups motivated Jesus to say, "They be blind leaders of the blind"?

ANSWERS

1. of life (John 6:35)
2. the birth of Jesus (Matthew 2:2; Luke 2:4–5; Luke 2:7)
3. He brought him back to life (Luke 7:14–15).
4. c (Revelation 22:20 NIV)
5. Pharisees and scribes (Matthew 15:1, 14 KJV)

Day 162

1. All the silver, gold, bronze, and iron in Jericho was
   a) used to improve the ark of the covenant.
   b) put into the Lord's treasury.
   c) used to build the Tower of Babel.
   d) made into fancy jewelry.

2. What leader of Israel had a staff, or rod, that turned into a snake?

3. Connect the Thoughts:
   camel
   vulture
   pig

4. What fishing tool did Jesus liken to the kingdom of heaven in a parable found only in Matthew's Gospel?

5. Match: Manna. . .
   a) twice a day, seven days a week
   b) once a day, six days a week
   c) once a day, seven days a week

ANSWERS

1. b (Joshua 6:19)
2. Moses (Exodus 4:1–4)
3. unclean animals (Leviticus 11:1–19)
4. a net (Matthew 13:47–50)
5. b (Exodus 16:21–26)

Day 163

1. Match: Adam and Eve. . .
    a) Adam made garments for Eve and himself.
    b) God made garments for them.
    c) Eve made garments out of animal skins.

2. What sin against the Holy Spirit, according to Jesus, would result in eternal guilt?

3. According to the apostle Paul, the wages of sin is what?
    a) disease
    b) pain
    c) death
    d) grief

4. Complete the scripture:
    "In your anger do not sin": Do not let the _____ _____ _____ while you are still angry.

5. We shouldn't be jealous of wicked people because they
    a) will have no reward.
    b) will be cursed.
    c) know the Lord.
    d) will gain weight from eating too much rich food.

ANSWERS

1. b (Genesis 3:21)
2. blasphemy (Mark 3:28–29)
3. c (Romans 6:23)
4. sun go down (Ephesians 4:26 NIV)
5. a (Proverbs 24:19–20 KJV)

Day 164

1. According to the Proverbs, a good name is what?
   a) better than great riches
   b) difficult to maintain
   c) the heritage of the Lord's children
   d) its own reward

2. What did Jesus tell His disciples to do to the people who cursed them?

3. Complete the scripture:
   Pride goeth before destruction, and an ___ spirit before a fall.

4. What, according to Hebrews, is the Word of God sharper than?
   a) a spear
   b) a flint
   c) a twoedged sword
   d) a thorn

5. What did Jesus promise God the Father would give to anyone who asked?

ANSWERS

1. a (Proverbs 22:1)
2. bless them (Luke 6:20, 28)
3. haughty (Proverbs 16:18 KJV)
4. c (Hebrews 4:12 KJV)
5. the Holy Spirit (Luke 11:11–13)

Day 165

1. Whom did Eve say "replaced" the murdered Abel?
    a) Seth
    b) Enosh
    c) Lamech
    d) Jared

2. How many languages appeared on the sign—reading JESUS OF NAZARETH THE KING OF THE JEWS—that hung on Jesus' cross?

3. Connect the Thoughts:
    the darts of the wicked
    the Christian's trials
    Nebuchadnezzar's furnace

4. Match: One hundred. . .
    a) in talents, what Sheba gave Solomon in gold
    b) in silver pieces, what Jacob paid for land in Canaan
    c) people killed by Samson at Lehi

5. The book of Ezra opens with
    a) Christ's birth.
    b) the end of the Jews' captivity in Babylon.
    c) a psalm of David.
    d) a prophecy about the end of the world.

ANSWERS

1. a (Genesis 4:25)
2. three (John 19:19–20)
3. fiery things (Ephesians 6:16; 1 Peter 4:12; Daniel 3:19–20)
4. b (Genesis 33:18–19 NIV)
5. b

Day 166

1. Although Jesus asked the woman at the well for water to drink, what kind of water did He offer to give her?

2. Match: Jesus. . .
   a) promised that the greatest on earth would be greatest in heaven.
   b) promised the Pharisees long life.
   c) promised disciples would one day sit on twelve thrones.

3. Isaiah prophesied that Jesus would be "a man of" what?
   a) joy
   b) sorrows
   c) power
   d) pain

4. Connect the Thoughts:
   "Man shall not live by bread alone, but by every word of God."
   "Thou shalt worship the Lord thy God, and him only shalt thou serve."
   "Thou shalt not tempt the Lord thy God."

5. When Jesus was on earth, on what two occasions did God speak directly from heaven?

ANSWERS

1. water "welling up to eternal life" (John 4:7–14 NIV)
2. c (Matthew 19:28)
3. b (Isaiah 53:3)
4. arguments Jesus used to battle Satan's temptation (Luke 4:1–13 KJV)
5. Jesus' baptism (Matthew 3:16–17); Jesus' transfiguration (Mark 9:1–7)

Day 167

1. What twin brother of Jacob was born hairy?

2. After he was grown, Moses fled Egypt because he
    a) stole from the treasury.
    b) was found to be a Hebrew.
    c) killed an Egyptian for smiting a Hebrew.
    d) killed a Hebrew for smiting a member of the royal court.

3. Connect the Thoughts:
    a woman named Zipporah
    a forty-year journey
    tablets of stone

4. Match: Aaron and Moses. . .
    a) Aaron had a speech impediment, so Moses talked to Pharaoh.
    b) Moses created a golden calf from the Hebrews' gold.
    c) Aaron's staff became a snake.

5. When God promised Abraham that his wife Sarah would have a baby, he
    a) praised God.
    b) invested in a college fund.
    c) bought a box of expensive cigars.
    d) laughed.

ANSWERS

1. Esau (Genesis 25:25–26)
2. c (Exodus 2:11–12, 15)
3. Moses (Exodus 2:21; Numbers 14:26–34; Exodus 31:18)
4. c (Exodus 7:10)
5. d (Genesis 17:16–17)

Day 168

1. What hostile army, pursuing the people of Israel, was completely destroyed in the middle of the Red Sea?

2. Connect the Thoughts:
   an axe head that floated
   bears that mauled mouthy kids
   a Shunammite boy raised from the dead

3. Match: The plague of blood. . .
   a) Egypt's magicians were unable to change water into blood.
   b) Aaron struck the Nile with his staff.
   c) Despite the plague, Egyptians could still drink the water.

4. What was Euroclydon?

5. What did the people of Malta say about Paul when a snakebite didn't kill him?
   a) that he was lucky
   b) that he was a demon
   c) that he was a god
   d) that he was really tough

ANSWERS

1. the Egyptians (Exodus 14:21–28, 15:4)
2. miracles of Elisha (2 Kings 6:1–7; 2 Kings 2:22–24; 2 Kings 4:32–37)
3. b (Exodus 7:19–20)
4. the name of a storm (Acts 27:14 KJV)
5. c (Acts 28:1–6)

Day 169

1. When God spoke to Moses, what name did the Lord use for Himself?

2. The Holy Spirit bears witness with us that we are what to God?

3. When did it happen that "God created the heavens and the earth"?
    a) Billions of years ago. . .
    b) In the fullness of time. . .
    c) In the beginning. . .
    d) From ancient times. . .

4. In addition to one body, one Spirit, one hope, one Lord, one faith, and one baptism, what else does Ephesians say we have one of?

5. The statement "For nothing is impossible with God" referred to what miracle?
    a) salvation for the Gentiles
    b) raising the dead
    c) the virgin birth of Jesus
    d) Elizabeth becoming a mother

ANSWERS

1. I AM and/or I AM THAT I AM (Exodus 3:14 KJV)
2. His children (Romans 8:16)
3. c (Genesis 1:1)
4. one God and Father (Ephesians 4:4–6)
5. d (Luke 1:36–37)

Day 170

1. What professional title, besides missionary, did Luke hold?

2. Connect the Thoughts:
   a brother of Jesus
   the Cyrenian who carried Jesus' cross
   a Canaanite disciple

3. Which New Testament writer says we are a holy priesthood, a royal priesthood?

4. Match: Rhoda. . .
   a) daughter of Herodias who danced at Herod's birthday
   b) sister of Laban
   c) servant who recognized Peter's voice

5. What devout Gentile received a visit from the angel of the Lord?

ANSWERS

1. doctor (Colossians 4:14)
2. men named Simon (Matthew 13:55; Matthew 27:32; Matthew 10:2–4)
3. Peter (1 Peter 2:5, 9)
4. c (Acts 12:13–14)
5. Cornelius (Acts 10:1–3)

Day 171

1. What town was home to Jesse's boys?

2. Match: Athens. . .
   a) where Paul spent his boyhood
   b) where Jason's house was located
   c) where Paul spoke of an idol to an unknown god

3. Where will the Lord live when He returns to earth?

4. King Ahab wanted the vineyard of Naboth the Jezreelite because
   a) it was near his palace and he wanted to use it as a vegetable garden.
   b) it was a perfect location to film his latest movie.
   c) he needed the land so he could build a temple to Baal.
   d) his goats needed more land for pasture.

5. Who alone could enter the Holy of Holies and on what occasion?

ANSWERS

1. Bethlehem (1 Samuel 17:58)
2. c (Acts 17:22–23)
3. Zion (Joel 3:21)
4. a (1 Kings 21:2)
5. the high priest on the Day of Atonement (Leviticus 16)

Day 172

1. Which of the following baking items did Jesus compare to the kingdom of heaven?
    a) a pan
    b) flour
    c) an egg
    d) yeast

2. Connect the Thoughts:
    water turned into wine
    a storm calmed
    ten lepers cleansed

3. What word is the Greek equivalent of *Messiah*?

4. Matthew says that the criminals crucified with Christ were
    a) murderers.
    b) tax collectors.
    c) thieves.
    d) all of the above.

5. Match: Immanuel. . .
    a) Jesus
    b) Isaiah
    c) Jeremiah

ANSWERS

1. d (Matthew 13:33 NIV)
2. miracles of Jesus (John 2:1–11; Matthew 8:23–27; Luke 17:11–19)
3. Christ
4. c (Matthew 27:44 KJV)
5. a (Matthew 1:23 NIV)

Day 173

1. What two animals represent the saved and lost people of earth, whom Jesus will separate at the final judgment?

2. Connect the Thoughts:
   Samson's snack of honey
   David's dangerous shepherd duty
   Jesus' title "of the tribe of Judah"

3. According to God, of what kind of wood was the ark to be made?

4. Match: Tabernacle bread. . .
   a) seven loaves
   b) ten loaves
   c) twelve loaves

5. What was engraved on the front of the high priest's turban?

ANSWERS

1. sheep and goats (Matthew 25:31–33)
2. lions (Judges 14:5–9; 1 Samuel 17:34–36; Revelation 5:5)
3. Gopher wood (Genesis 6:14 KJV)
4. c (Leviticus 24:3–5)
5. a gold plate was engraved with HOLINESS TO THE LORD (Exodus 28:36–38 KJV)

Day 174

1. According to the Proverbs, a prostitute reduces a man to what?
    a) a brute beast
    b) a blind beggar
    c) a blemished bull
    d) a piece of bread

2. What "lake" is the final, eternal home for those people whose names are not found in the book of life?

3. Connect the Thoughts:
    Abimelech's demise
    forbidden as pledge for a debt
    punishment for causing a child to sin

4. What happened to the prophet who ate and drank when God told him not to?

5. What was the apostle Paul's rule toward people who refused to work?
    a) They should be prayed over.
    b) They should not eat.
    c) They should be disciplined by the church.
    d) They should not expect charity.

ANSWERS

1. d (Proverbs 6:20, 26 KJV)
2. the lake of fire (Revelation 20:15)
3. millstones (Judges 9:52–53; Deuteronomy 24:6; Matthew 18:6)
4. A lion killed him (1 Kings 13:20–24).
5. b (2 Thessalonians 3:10)

Day 175

1. John says that when someone pretends to be a Christian but really isn't, you should
   a) not let the person into your house.
   b) pretend you don't speak English.
   c) spread the blood of a lamb on your door.
   d) tell everybody you know.

2. What, along with godliness, did the apostle Paul tell Timothy "is great gain"?

3. Jesus says He will give His believers what two *W* words when we are brought before our adversaries on account of His name?

4. Throughout his first letter, John tells Christians not to love
   a) their brothers.
   b) pagans.
   c) television.
   d) the world.

5. If we show love only to those who love us, we are no better than whom?

ANSWERS

1. a (2 John 1:7–10)
2. contentment (1 Timothy 6:6 NIV)
3. words and wisdom (Luke 21:15 NIV)
4. d (1 John 2:15)
5. Jesus says we are no better than the publicans, or tax collectors, some of the most hated people of His time (Matthew 5:46–47).

Day 176

1. What did the Philistines, envious of Isaac's wealth in flocks and herds, try to destroy?

2. Connect the Thoughts:
    merry
    deceitful
    hardened

3. Whose name means "morning star" or "son of the morning"?

4. Match: Fifty-two. . .
    a) days Nehemiah spent rebuilding Jerusalem's wall
    b) days Jesus fasted in the wilderness
    c) messengers Jesus sent out as missionaries

5. What kind of tree caught Absalom's head as he rode underneath on a mule, leaving him hanging?

ANSWERS

1. wells (Genesis 26:12–15)
2. kinds of hearts (Proverbs 17:22 KJV; Jeremiah 17:9; Exodus 7:14 KJV)
3. Lucifer (Isaiah 14:12)
4. a (Nehemiah 2:17, 6:15)
5. oak (2 Samuel 18:9–10)

Day 177

1. How many years, according to John's Revelation, will Jesus reign on earth before Satan's final judgment?

2. Connect the Thoughts:
   Word of God
   Lamb of God
   Son of God

3. Why was Jesus in Jerusalem when He got separated from His parents?

4. How long did Jesus' parents search before they found Him?

5. How many siblings, the natural children of Mary and Joseph, did Jesus have?
   a) none
   b) two
   c) four
   d) six or more

ANSWERS

1. one thousand (Revelation 20:6–10)
2. titles of Jesus Christ (Revelation 19:13–16; John 1:29; Mark 1:1)
3. Feast of the Passover (Luke 2:39–43)
4. three days (Luke 2:46)
5. d (Mark 6:3)

Day 178

1. Abraham's servant gave Rebekah
   a) a Happy Meal.
   b) three sheep.
   c) silver jewelry.
   d) gold jewelry.

2. What woman, the wife of Elkanah, was mother of the prophet Samuel?

3. What prophet went into depression when the evil Queen Jezebel threatened his life?
   a) Isaiah
   b) Nathan
   c) Samuel
   d) Elijah

4. Connect the Thoughts:
   a young protégé
   wicked sons
   a broken neck

5. Match: Joseph and his brothers. . .
   a) Joseph had his own silver cup placed in Benjamin's sack.
   b) Reuben asked to stay in Egypt in place of Benjamin.
   c) Joseph's brothers sold him for thirty shekels to Midianite merchants.

ANSWERS

1. d (Genesis 24:1–2, 10–22)
2. Hannah (1 Samuel 1:19–20)
3. d (1 Kings 19:1–4)
4. Eli the priest (1 Samuel 2:11–12; 1 Samuel 4:16–18)
5. a (Genesis 44:1–2, 12)

Day 179

1. True or False: Mary and Joseph had been married for twenty years before she became pregnant by the Holy Spirit.

2. To divide the Red Sea, Moses lifted
   a) the belt of his robe.
   b) both hands.
   c) the name of the Lord.
   d) his hand and his rod.

3. Connect the Thoughts:
   a centurion named Julius
   Euroclydon
   a shipwreck

4. True or False: Elisha told the kings to build ditches in a dry stream bed.

5. What young king removed all the mediums and spiritists from Judah, as required in the book of the law found by his priest, Hilkiah?

ANSWERS

1. False
2. d (Exodus 14:15–16, 21)
3. the apostle Paul's journey to Rome (Acts 27:1–44)
4. True (2 Kings 3:13–16)
5. Josiah (2 Kings 22:1–8, 23:24–25)

Day 180

1. When Jesus said He is the "true vine," who does He say is the gardener?

2. What famous Bible personality did God name "Jedidiah"?
   a) Noah
   b) Solomon
   c) Jeremiah
   d) Daniel

3. What does God say in Genesis 6:3 (KJV) that His Spirit will not always do?

4. True or False: As part of His covenant with Abraham, God wanted Abraham and his descendants to worship Him.

5. God tells us to honor our
   a) pastor.
   b) friends.
   c) father and mother.
   d) teachers and principal.

ANSWERS

1. His Father (John 15:1)
2. b (2 Samuel 12:24–25)
3. strive with men
4. True (Genesis 17:7)
5. c (Exodus 20:12; Deuteronomy 5:16)

Day 181

1. What servant of the high priest had his ear sliced off by Peter's sword—then restored by Jesus—during Jesus' arrest?

2. Connect the Thoughts:
   Ananias
   Caiaphas
   Jesus Christ

3. What high priest did Paul call a whitewashed wall?

4. Match: Phoebe. . .
   a) wife of Felix
   b) servant or deaconess of the early church
   c) wife of Herod Agrippa

5. Which disciple brought the boy with the five loaves and two fish to Jesus?

ANSWERS

1. Malchus (Luke 22:50–5; John 18:10)
2. high priests (Acts 23:2; John 18:13; Hebrews 3:1)
3. Ananias (Acts 23:2–3 NIV)
4. b (Romans 16:1)
5. Andrew (John 6:8–9)

Day 182

1. What wicked city did Jesus pair with Sodom?

2. Connect the Thoughts:
   Pergamos
   Sardis
   Philadelphia

3. What town, along with Bethsaida, did not repent when Jesus performed miracles there and thus received a pronouncement of woe?

4. Match: Valley of Sorek. . .
   a) where Samuel anointed David
   b) where Samson fell in love with Delilah
   c) where Ruth fell in love with Boaz

5. The book of Nahum prophesies the fall of what city?
   a) Babylon
   b) Tyre
   c) Susa
   d) Nineveh

ANSWERS

1. Gomorrah (Matthew 10:15)
2. churches of Revelation (Revelation 2:12 KJV; Revelation 3:1; Revelation 3:7)
3. Korazin, or Chorazin (Matthew 11:20–21)
4. b (Judges 16:1–4)
5. d (Nahum 1:1)

Day 183

1. To whom did Jesus say, "Every. . .house divided against itself shall not stand"?

2. Match: Wonderful Counselor. . .
   a) first used by Jeremiah
   b) first used by Isaiah
   c) first used in the Psalms by David

3. How many criminals were crucified with Jesus at Golgotha?

4. Connect the Thoughts:
   midday darkness
   a centurion praising God
   "Into thy hands I commend my spirit."

5. Who are the four women mentioned in Jesus' genealogy in Matthew 1 (NIV)?

ANSWERS

1. the Pharisees (Matthew 12:24–25 KJV)
2. b (Isaiah 9:6)
3. two (Mark 15:22, 27)
4. Jesus' death (Luke 23:44–47 KJV)
5. Tamar, Rahab, Ruth, Bathsheba ("Uriah's wife")

Day 184

1. What type of tree does the love-smitten woman of the Song of Solomon compare her man to?

2. What metal, used to sharpen other like metal, does Proverbs compare to friends?

3. Connect the Thoughts:
   Amos' vision of a basket
   love, joy, peace, etc.
   the tree of the knowledge of good and evil

4. What herbs did Jesus say the Pharisees tithed?

5. What part of a dead donkey did Samson use to kill one thousand enemy Philistines?

ANSWERS

1. apple (Song of Solomon 2:3)
2. iron (Proverbs 27:17)
3. fruit (Amos 8:1; Galatians 5:22–23; Genesis 2:17, 3:3)
4. mint, anise, and cummin (Matthew 23:23 KJV)
5. a jawbone (Judges 15:14–16)

Day 185

1. Who was stoned to death after admitting he had stolen clothing, silver, and gold from the ruins of Jericho?

2. The unrepentant criminal who was crucified with Jesus asked Him to
   a) turn stones into bread.
   b) ask a centurion for a cup of water.
   c) bless him and his family.
   d) save Himself and them.

3. In asking for this, the unrepentant criminal was asking Jesus to prove what?

4. Connect the Thoughts:
   a proud look
   a lying tongue
   hands that shed innocent blood

5. What prophet got so angry at God that he told God to just go ahead and kill him?

ANSWERS

1. Achan (Joshua 7:19–25)
2. d (Luke 23:39)
3. that He is the Christ (Luke 23:39)
4. things the Lord hates (Proverbs 6:16–19)
5. Jonah (Jonah 4:1–3)

Day 186

1. What piece of the armor of God can quench the fiery darts or flaming arrows of Satan?

2. John says that true Christians have
   a) love.
   b) fear.
   c) gold plaques with their names engraved on them.
   d) money invested in John's real estate firm.

3. What does Jesus say the angels do when one sinner repents?

4. True or False: We don't have to forgive anybody who doesn't ask us for forgiveness.

5. When Jesus speaks of neighbors, He means
   a) the people who live in the house next to yours.
   b) everyone.
   c) the people who live in your town.
   d) your enemies.

ANSWERS

1. the shield of faith (Ephesians 6:16 KJV)
2. a (1 John 2:5)
3. they rejoice; there is joy (Luke 15:10)
4. False (Luke 6:37)
5. b

Day 187

1. What musical instrument accompanies the song of victorious saints in heaven, according to John's Revelation?

2. Connect the Thoughts:
   Saul on the road to Damascus
   men of Sodom, at Lot's house
   Bartimaeus

3. What would King Xerxes hold out to show favor to the people who pleased him?

4. Match: Fourteen. . .
   a) generations from Babylonian exile to birth of Jesus
   b) days Jesus was tempted by Satan in the desert
   c) months Paul spent on Malta

5. Who killed two people at once with one spear?

ANSWERS

1. harps (Revelation 15:1–4)
2. blind people (Acts 9:3–8; Genesis 19:1–11; Mark 10:46)
3. a golden scepter (Esther 3:12, 4:11, 5:2)
4. a (Matthew 1:17)
5. Phinehas (Numbers 25:7–8)

Day 188

1. How did the soldiers at Golgotha decide who should receive Jesus' clothing?

2. Connect the Thoughts:
   Matthat
   Heli
   Joseph

3. When the disciples asked Jesus to tell them the signs of His coming and the end of the age, what prophet did Jesus quote?

4. Complete the scripture:
   God made him who had no ____ to be ____ for us, so that in him we might become the righteousness of God.

5. Match: How Jesus became the Nazarene. . .
   a) Joseph was told to go to Nazareth in a dream.
   b) Simeon told Joseph to go to Nazareth.
   c) Zechariah told Joseph to go to Nazareth.

ANSWERS

1. by casting lots (John 19:23–24)
2. the family line of Jesus (Luke 3:23–24)
3. Daniel (Matthew 24:3, 15)
4. sin, sin (2 Corinthians 5:21 NIV)
5. a (Matthew 2:19–23)

Day 189

1. What Bible strongman lost his power when his long hair was cut off?

2. What Old Testament leader overcame a huge enemy army, "like grasshoppers for multitude," with three hundred men handpicked by God Himself?
   a) Samson
   b) Gideon
   c) David
   d) Saul

3. What judge of Israel made a foolish vow that cost him the life of his only daughter?

4. Connect the Thoughts:
   Elijah
   Haggai
   Daniel

5. Match: Cain and Abel. . .
   a) Abel worked the soil while Cain tended the sheep.
   b) Abel was sentenced by God to wander the earth.
   c) Cain was sent to live east of Eden.

ANSWERS

1. Samson (Judges 16:15–20)
2. b (Judges 7:1–25 KJV)
3. Jephthah (Judges 11:30–39)
4. prophets (1 Kings 18:36; Haggai 2:1; Matthew 24:15)
5. c (Genesis 4:16)

Day 190

1. After Goliath died, the Israelites
   a) chased the Philistines back to their own country.
   b) offered the Philistines a permanent peace treaty.
   c) slept.
   d) sang "I'm in the Lord's Army!"

2. What event in Jesus' life featured a voice from heaven saying, "This is my Son, whom I love"?

3. Connect the Thoughts:
   an abundance of frogs
   three days of darkness
   the death of firstborn sons

4. Complete the scripture:
   "Take off your sandals, for the place you are standing is ____ ____."

5. The Feast of the Tabernacles commemorated
   a) Jesus' birth in a stable.
   b) the building of Solomon's temple.
   c) the forty years' wandering in the wilderness.
   d) the Mormon Tabernacle Choir.

ANSWERS

1. a (1 Samuel 17:4, 51–52)
2. His baptism (Matthew 3:16–17 NIV)
3. plagues on Egypt (Exodus 8:3; Exodus 10:21–22; Exodus 11:5)
4. holy, ground (Exodus 3:5)
5. c (Leviticus 23:33–43)

Day 191

1. To whom did Jesus say, "My Father is always at his work to this very day, and I too am working"?

2. Which of the following does the Bible say God keeps numbered?
   a) the hairs of your head
   b) the trees of the forest
   c) the fish of the sea
   d) the burgers served at McDonald's

3. What are five symbols of the Holy Spirit?

4. God tells us not to covet other people's possessions. That means we should not
   a) steal from our friends.
   b) destroy other people's belongings.
   c) make fun of others.
   d) wish we had our neighbor's stuff.

5. What fourteen-letter word defined the ministry that Paul told the Corinthians God has given those who are in Christ?

ANSWERS

1. the Jews at the temple (John 5:16–17 NIV)
2. a (Matthew 10:30)
3. water (John 7:38–39), wind or Spirit (John 3:8), seal (Ephesians 1:13), dove (Matthew 3:16), fire (Acts 2:3–4)
4. d
5. reconciliation (2 Corinthians 5:18)

Day 192

1. What wicked New Testament king "was eaten by worms and died" for allowing people to call him a god?

2. Connect the Thoughts:
   Aristarchus
   Tychicus
   Aquila and Priscilla

3. What mother-to-be made this statement? "My soul glorifies the Lord and my spirit rejoices in God my Savior."

4. How many descriptions are given of Judas Iscariot's death?

5. What was Pontius Pilate's job?

ANSWERS

1. Herod (Acts 12:21–23 NIV)
2. coworkers with the apostle Paul (Colossians 4:10; Colossians 4:7; Romans 16:3)
3. Mary (Luke 1:30–33, 46–47 NIV)
4. two (Matthew 27:5; Acts 1:18)
5. governor of Judea (Luke 3:1)

Day 193

1. What sea was the location of Jesus' calling of Peter and Andrew?

2. Match: Bethel. . .
   a) where Lazarus lived
   b) where a pool existed known for its healing powers
   c) where Jacob built an altar

3. Where did Paul meet Aquila and Priscilla?

4. Naboth refused to let King Ahab have his vineyard because
   a) he had lost the deed to the land in a Monopoly game.
   b) the land belonged to his mother-in-law.
   c) the land was not good enough for the glorious King Ahab.
   d) God refused to let him give King Ahab the land.

5. What separated the Holy Place from the Most Holy Place?

ANSWERS

1. Galilee (Matthew 4:18–19)
2. c (Genesis 35:1)
3. Corinth (Acts 18:1–2)
4. d (1 Kings 21:1–3)
5. a veil or curtain (Exodus 26:33)

Day 194

1. From what mountain did Jesus talk about the end times?

2. Complete Jesus' sentence: "The Son of Man did not come to be served, but to serve, and to give his life as a ____ for many."

3. What "amazed" Jesus about the people of His hometown?

4. Connect the Thoughts:
   "The Son of man hath not where to lay his head."
   "Let the dead bury their dead."
   "No man, having put his hand to the plough, and looking back, is fit for the kingdom of God."

5. Whom does the author of Hebrews trust?

ANSWERS

1. Mount of Olives (Matthew 24:3)
2. ransom (Matthew 20:28 NIV)
3. their lack of faith (Mark 6:4–6)
4. Jesus' comments to people who said they wanted to follow Him (Matthew 8:20 KJV; Matthew 8:22 KJV; Luke 9:62 KJV)
5. Jesus (Hebrews 2:9, 13)

Day 195

1. What kind of animal was the "prodigal son" feeding when he realized he should return home to his father?

2. Connect the Thoughts:
   wild goat
   leviathan
   behemoth

3. Match: Eagle feathers. . .
   a) what Nebuchadnezzar wore in his crown
   b) what Nebuchadnezzar's hair looked like, to fulfill his dream
   c) what Nebuchadnezzar collected

4. What gem "of great value" did Jesus mention in a parable found only in Matthew's Gospel?

5. What was the "forbidden fruit" that Adam and Eve ate?
   a) an apple
   b) a fig
   c) a pear
   d) it's not specified

ANSWERS

1. pigs (Luke 15:11–20)
2. creatures in the book of Job (Job 39:1 KJV; Job 41:1; Job 40:15)
3. b (Daniel 4:33)
4. pearl (Matthew 13:45–46)
5. d (Genesis 3:6)

Day 196

1. What Old Testament prophet had to buy back his adulterous wife with silver and barley?

2. What was the name of the above-mentioned prophet's wife?
   a) Abigail
   b) Gomer
   c) Tamar
   d) Tryphena

3. What punishment did God give humankind because their every thought was "evil continually"?

4. Connect the Thoughts:
   fornicators
   idolators
   thieves

5. According to the Proverbs, what is true of an adulterous woman's speech?
   a) It is smoother than oil.
   b) It has ensnared many young men.
   c) It is full of lies.
   d) It can confuse the wise.

ANSWERS

1. Hosea (Hosea 3:1–2)
2. b (Hosea 1:3)
3. the flood (Genesis 6 KJV)
4. people who won't inherit the kingdom of God (1 Corinthians 6:9–10 KJV)
5. a (Proverbs 5:3)

Day 197

1. What troublesome desire did Paul say is "common to man"?

2. Connect the Thoughts:
   a house built on rock
   new wine in old bottles
   an unmerciful servant

3. No branch can bear fruit unless it does what?

4. Regarding enemies, Jesus said we are to
   a) love them.
   b) bless them.
   c) pray for them.
   d) all of the above.

5. According to Jesus, people will know we are His disciples when we
   a) get three perfect attendance pins at church.
   b) love one another.
   c) go to Vacation Bible School every year.
   d) listen to Christian radio stations every day.

ANSWERS

1. temptation (1 Corinthians 10:13 NIV)
2. parables of Jesus (Matthew 7:24–27; Mark 2:19–22; Matthew 18:21–35)
3. remain in the vine (John 15:4)
4. d (Matthew 5:43–44 KJV)
5. b (John 13:34–35)

Day 198

1. What kind of cakes did Abigail take to King David to apologize for her husband's rude behavior?

2. Connect the Thoughts:
   the selection of Matthias as an apostle
   soldiers competing for the crucified Jesus' clothing
   Jonah determined as the cause of a storm at sea

3. Match: Seven. . .
   a) banquets Esther hosted for Haman and Xerxes
   b) times Shunammite's son sneezed after Elisha restored his life
   c) coins widow deposited in temple treasury

4. True or False: Both criminals who were crucified with Jesus thought He was guilty of the crimes with which He was charged.

5. According to the Proverbs, "a good name is" what?
   a) better than great riches
   b) difficult to maintain
   c) the heritage of the Lord's children
   d) its own reward

ANSWERS

1. fig (1 Samuel 25:18–25 KJV)
2. the casting of lots (Acts 1:26; Matthew 27:27, 35; Jonah 1:4–7)
3. b (2 Kings 4:35–36)
4. False (Luke 23:39–41)
5. a (Proverbs 22:1)

Day 199

1. What did mocking soldiers offer Jesus to drink while He hung on the cross at Golgotha?

2. Connect the Thoughts:
   go into all the world
   teach all nations
   baptize

3. When the chief priests and elders demanded to know by what authority Jesus taught, what question did Jesus use to confound them?

4. According to the apostle John, "Everyone who believes that Jesus is the Messiah is born of ____."

5. Paul writes to the Romans, "The night is nearly over; the day is almost here." What does he mean by "the day"?

ANSWERS

1. vinegar, or wine mixed with myrrh (Luke 23:36; Mark 15:23)
2. Jesus' "Great Commission" (Matthew 28:18–20)
3. "John's baptism—where did it come from? Was it from heaven, or from men?" (Matthew 21:23–25 NIV).
4. God (1 John 5:1 NIV)
5. the time of Jesus' return (Romans 13:12 NIV)

Day 200

1. Joseph's father loved him more than any of his other children because Joseph
   a) was the child of his old age.
   b) was handsome.
   c) had good taste in clothes.
   d) showered him with gold, frankincense, and myrrh.

2. What man lived the longest life recorded in the Bible—969 years?

3. When Miriam is first mentioned by name in the Bible, she is
   a) drinking wine.
   b) celebrating the Israelites' victory over the Canaanites.
   c) leading the women in song and dance.
   d) predicting good tidings for Israel.

4. Connect the Thoughts:
   shepherd
   harpist
   king

5. Match: Absalom, Amnon, and Tamar. . .
   a) Amnon fell in love with his half sister Tamar.
   b) Absalom banished Amnon from Israel.
   c) Absalom killed himself out of shame for his sister.

ANSWERS

1. a (Genesis 37:3)
2. Methuselah (Genesis 5:27)
3. c (Exodus 15:20)
4. David (1 Samuel 16:11–13; 1 Samuel 16:23; 2 Samuel 2:4)
5. a (2 Samuel 13:1)

Day 201

1. What miracle occurred in the heavens the day Joshua and the Israelites defeated the armies of the Amorites?

2. When Mary Magdalene first saw the empty tomb, she
   a) rejoiced.
   b) was angry.
   c) questioned the guards.
   d) wept.

3. True or False: Elisha purified a pot of stew that contained poisonous gourds.

4. Connect the Thoughts:
   a donkey and a colt
   clothes and branches on the roadway
   people shouting, "Hosanna!"

5. Why did David visit the Israelites' battlefield?

ANSWERS

1. the sun stood still (Joshua 10:9–14)
2. d (John 20:1, 11)
3. True (2 Kings 4:38-41)
4. Jesus' triumphal entry into Jerusalem (Matthew 21:1–11)
5. David was taking food to his three older brothers who were soldiers in battle (1 Samuel 17:13, 17–18).

Day 202

1. What protective structures, which proved inadequate for Jericho, did God warn Israel against trusting in?

2. True or False: When you pray, you should always give thanks to God.

3. According to the prophet Joel, what would the Holy Spirit enable young men and young women to do?

4. According to the apostle Paul, the Christian's body is the what of the Holy Spirit?
   a) temple
   b) house
   c) chariot
   d) slave

5. What two words describe the throne on which God sits while passing final judgment on those who have died?

ANSWERS

1. walls (Deuteronomy 28:52)
2. True
3. see visions, prophesy (Joel 2:28–32; Acts 2:16–21)
4. a (1 Corinthians 6:19)
5. great white (Revelation 20:11–13)

Day 203

1. What New Testament preacher, like the Old Testament hero Samson, was never to drink wine or other fermented drink?

2. What two disciples from Jesus' inner circle, described as "unschooled, ordinary men," amazed the Jewish leaders with their courage in preaching the gospel?

3. Connect the Thoughts:
   husband Zechariah
   son John
   cousin Mary

4. What was the occupation of the Ethiopian eunuch in Acts 8?

5. What two groups of philosophers questioned Paul in Athens?

ANSWERS

1. John the Baptist (Judges 13:5, 24; Luke 1:13–15)
2. Peter and John (Acts 4:1–20)
3. Elizabeth (Luke 1:5 NIV; Luke 1:57–60 NIV; Luke 1:34–37 NIV)
4. treasurer (Acts 8:27)
5. Epicureans and Stoics (Acts 17:18 NIV)

Day 204

1. What kind of place was Patmos, where John received his revelation of Jesus Christ?

2. Connect the Thoughts:
   Achor
   Hinnom
   the shadow of death

3. What river connects the Sea of Galilee with the Dead Sea?

4. Match: Cenchrea. . .
   a) where Ur was located
   b) where Paul shaved his head
   c) region named after Caesar Augustus

5. Where did Abraham find a ram to sacrifice after God stopped him from sacrificing his son Isaac?

ANSWERS

1. island (Revelation 1:9)
2. valleys (Joshua 7:26; Joshua 18:16; Psalm 23:4)
3. the Jordan River
4. b (Acts 18:18)
5. thicket (Genesis 22:9–13)

Day 205

1. Connect the Thoughts:
    a napkin
    linen clothes
    an empty tomb

2. What religious group did Jesus twice call a "brood (or generation) of vipers"?

3. Who wove the crown of thorns that Jesus wore?
    a) Pontius Pilate
    b) Caiaphas, the high priest
    c) Herod
    d) Roman soldiers

4. While Jesus had given the disciples authority to perform miracles in His name, what did He want them to rejoice about instead?

5. Match: Jesus' clearing of the temple. . .
    a) on the same day as the triumphal entry
    b) on the same day as the Olivet Discourse
    c) on the day after the triumphal entry

ANSWERS

1. the resurrection of Jesus (John 20:1–9 KJV)
2. the Pharisees (Matthew 12:24–34, 23:29–33)
3. d (John 19:2)
4. that their names were written in heaven (Luke 10:19–20)
5. c (Mark 11:1–17)

Day 206

1. What was Saul looking for when he learned he would become the king of Israel?
   a) a wife
   b) lost donkeys
   c) water
   d) a job

2. What insect made a large part of the diet of John the Baptist?

3. Connect the Thoughts:
   corruptible versus incorruptible
   Jesus' thorns
   cast before God's throne

4. What two animals did David boast of killing?

5. Which of the following is not a food the Israelites craved from Egypt?
   a) cucumbers
   b) melons
   c) onions
   d) apples

ANSWERS

1. b (1 Samuel 10:1–2)
2. locusts (Matthew 3:4)
3. crowns (1 Corinthians 9:25; John 19:5; Revelation 4:10–11)
4. bear, lion (1 Samuel 17:34–36)
5. d (Numbers 11:5)

Day 207

1. What sin was a woman caught in by scribes and Pharisees who then tried to trick Jesus into approving her death by stoning?

2. True or False: The Lord called Aaron and Miriam into the tabernacle to chasten them for speaking against Moses.

3. What were Barabbas' crimes?

4. What group of people, according to the apostle Paul, might "learn to be idle" and turn away from God?
   a) young widows
   b) the rich
   c) old men
   d) children

5. Complete the scripture:
   Jesus says of the man who betrayed the Son of Man, "It would be better for him if ________________."

ANSWERS

1. adultery (John 8:1–11)
2. True (Numbers 12:5–8)
3. robbery (John 18:40), insurrection/sedition, and murder (Mark 15:7; Luke 23:18–19)
4. a (1 Timothy 5:11–15 KJV)
5. he had not been born (Matthew 26:24 NIV)

Day 208

1. What "visual aid" did Jesus use to answer the disciples' question, "Who is the greatest in the kingdom of heaven?"

2. What two *S* words complete this scripture?
Take the helmet of ____ and the sword of the ____.

3. Complete this quotation of Jesus: "Foxes have dens, and birds have nests, but the Son of Man. . ."
   a) "has a beautiful palace in heaven."
   b) "has a small home in Jerusalem."
   c) "has no place to lay his head."
   d) "has twelve disciples to live with."

4. True or False: The disciples always understood the parables without Jesus having to explain them.

5. What question was Jesus answering when He told the parable of the good Samaritan?

ANSWERS

1. a child (Matthew 18:1–4)
2. salvation, Spirit (Ephesians 6:17)
3. c (Matthew 8:20 NIV)
4. False (Matthew 13:36)
5. "And who is my neighbour?" (Luke 10:29–37 KJV)

Day 209

1. What did Jesus eat in the presence of His disciples shortly after His resurrection?

2. Connect the Thoughts:
   Abib
   Adar
   Elul

3. What kind of fire does the prophet Malachi say the Lord will be like in the day of judgment?

4. Match: Deborah. . .
   a) wife of Barak
   b) held court under the Palm of Deborah
   c) sister of Jael, Sisera's slayer

5. What does Ebenezer mean?

ANSWERS

1. broiled fish (Luke 24:36–43)
2. months of the Hebrew calendar (Exodus 13:4; Esther 3:7; Nehemiah 6:15)
3. refiner's (Malachi 3:1–2)
4. b (Judges 4:4–5)
5. "stone of help" (1 Samuel 7:12)

Day 210

1. What animal feeding trough served as a temporary bed for the newborn Jesus?

2. What did John the Baptist say he was unworthy of doing for Christ?
   a) bearing His name
   b) untying His sandals
   c) performing His ministry
   d) cooking His supper

3. How did John the Baptist address Jesus when he saw Him by the Jordan?

4. After the Sabbath, what did Salome, Mary Magdalene, and Mary the mother of James take to the tomb of Jesus?
   a) spices
   b) burial linens
   c) olive branches and flowers
   d) marker of stones for His tomb

5. In the middle of a fierce storm, what did Jesus say to the wind and the waves?

ANSWERS

1. a manger (Luke 2:4–11)
2. b (Luke 3:16)
3. Lamb of God (John 1:29)
4. a (Mark 16:1)
5. "Quiet! Be still!" (Mark 4:39 NIV)

Day 211

1. What king of Tyre supplied cedar logs to Solomon for building the Lord's temple?

2. How old was Joseph when, after years of imprisonment on false charges, he rose to become second-in-command of Egypt?
   a) Eighteen years old
   b) Thirty years old
   c) Fifty years old
   d) Ninety years old

3. What widowed woman left her mother-in-law, Naomi, and sister-in-law, Ruth, to return to her homeland of Moab?

4. Connect the Thoughts:
   a priest in Nehemiah's day
   a warrior in David's army
   the weeping prophet

5. Match: Jonathan. . .
   a) He thrust his sword into his father, Saul, as he was dying.
   b) He warned David to flee by shooting arrows.
   c) His disabled son, Mephibosheth, was refused a place at David's table.

ANSWERS

1. Hiram (1 Kings 5:1–12)
2. b (Genesis 41:14–46)
3. Orpah (Ruth 1:3–5, 14–15)
4. men named Jeremiah (Nehemiah 12:1; 1 Chronicles 12:1–4; Jeremiah 13:17)
5. b (1 Samuel 20:35–42)

Day 212

1. When the local people found out that Jesus had driven the mob of demons out of a man, they
   a) feasted for a week.
   b) were afraid.
   c) composed a song in His honor.
   d) made Jesus the town's mayor.

2. Where were the Israelites to apply some of the blood from the Passover sacrifice?

3. Connect the Thoughts:
   the captain of the host of the Lord
   Joshua
   walking around a city for seven days

4. Who led the victory song after the Egyptians were drowned in the Red Sea?

5. During the Feast of the Tabernacles, native Israelites were instructed to live in
   a) stables.
   b) the temple.
   c) booths.
   d) choir lofts.

ANSWERS

1. b (Mark 5:15; Luke 8:35)
2. to their doorframes (Exodus 12:7, 11–13)
3. the fall of Jericho (Joshua 5:13–6:5 KJV)
4. Miriam (Exodus 15:19–20)
5. c (Leviticus 23:34, 42–43)

Day 213

1. What was the name of the altar that Moses built after the battle where he had to hold up his hands in order for the army to prevail?

2. Complete the scripture:
   Thy word is a ___ unto my feet.

3. According to Psalm 19, what of the Lord's are true and righteous?

4. True or False: God said to let poor people win lawsuits because they are poor.

5. According to Paul, what will we not fulfill if we walk in the Spirit?

ANSWERS

1. Jehovahnissi—The Lord Is My Banner (Exodus 17:10–15)
2. lamp (Psalm 119:105 KJV)
3. judgments (Psalm 19:9 KJV)
4. False (Exodus 23:2–3)
5. the lust of the flesh (Galatians 5:16 KJV)

Day 214

1. What imprisoned preacher sent his own disciples to Jesus to ask if He was the expected Messiah?

2. Connect the Thoughts:
   He lied to the apostles.
   He restored Saul's sight.
   He ordered the apostle Paul struck.

3. What did Zacchaeus do so that he could see Jesus?

4. Match: Herodias. . .
   a) was married to Herod.
   b) had a daughter who was asked to dance on Herod's birthday.
   c) was married to Herod Antipas.

5. In what town did Martha live?

ANSWERS

1. John the Baptist (Matthew 11:1–15)
2. men named Ananias (Acts 5:1–5; Acts 9:17–19; Acts 23:1–2)
3. He climbed a tree (Luke 19:2–4).
4. b (Matthew 14:6)
5. Bethany (John 11:1)

Day 215

1. What modern-day nation, with its capital at New Delhi, marked the eastern extent of King Xerxes' nation?

2. Connect the Thoughts:
   Magog
   Babylon
   Armageddon

3. On what mountain is the Garden of Gethsemane located?

4. Match: Zered Valley. . .
   a) where Moses led the Israelites after thirty-eight years of wandering
   b) where the Israelites defeated the Moabites
   c) where the Israelites defeated the Ammonites

5. What was the name of the valley from which came the word *Gehenna*, or "hell," where children were sacrificed by fire to pagan gods?

ANSWERS

1. India (Esther 8:9)
2. places in the book of Revelation (Revelation 20:7–8; Revelation 17:5; Revelation 16:16)
3. Mount of Olives
4. a (Deuteronomy 2:13–14 NIV)
5. Valley of Hinnom (2 Kings 23:10)

Day 216

1. Why did Joseph and Mary take Jesus to Jerusalem when He was twelve years old?

2. To which of the following did Jesus not liken the kingdom of heaven?
   a) a fish net
   b) a wedding banquet
   c) a fire
   d) a hidden treasure

3. In Matthew 5:17, what did Jesus say He came to do to the law and prophets?

4. Match: Branch. . .
   a) so named by Isaiah
   b) so named by Jeremiah
   c) so named by Daniel

5. In what parable did Jesus tell the chief priests and elders that publicans and harlots would enter the kingdom of God before they did?

ANSWERS

1. to celebrate the Feast of the Passover (Luke 2:41–42)
2. c (Matthew 13:44, 47, 22:2)
3. fulfill them (Matthew 5:17)
4. b (Jeremiah 23:5)
5. the parable of the two sons (Matthew 21:31 KJV)

Day 217

1. What insect swarmed Egypt in the fourth plague on Pharaoh—but stayed out of the land of Goshen where God's people lived?

2. Connect the Thoughts:
   mite
   farthing
   penny

3. When Noah got off the ark, what did he plant?

4. What type of bird does God say Ephraim—the nation of Israel—is like?

5. When God compared Israel to this bird, He meant Israel was
   a) strong and true.
   b) soaring upward.
   c) soft and feathery.
   d) flitting from place to place.

ANSWERS

1. flies (Exodus 8:20–24)
2. types of money (Mark 12:42 KJV; Luke 12:6 KJV; Matthew 22:19 KJV)
3. a vineyard (Genesis 8:16–18, 9:20)
4. a silly dove (Hosea 7:11–12)
5. d (Hosea 7:12)

Day 218

1. What does Numbers 32:23 say will happen if you sin?

2. What fellow worker did the apostle Paul say "hath forsaken me, having loved this present world"?
   a) Demas
   b) Tychicus
   c) Luke
   d) Epaphroditus

3. In addition to betraying Jesus, what other crime did Judas Iscariot commit?

4. True or False: Jesus teaches that when people say mean things to you or about you, you should be kind to them anyway.

5. What was the name of the evil spirit that possessed the man who lived in the tombs?

ANSWERS

1. You will be found out.
2. a (2 Timothy 4:10)
3. theft (John 12:4–6)
4. True (Matthew 5:44–45)
5. Legion (Mark 5:2–9)

Day 219

1. What does the apostle Paul urge Christians to be
". . .of God"?

2. Complete the scripture:
If any of you lack ____, let him ask of God. . .and it shall be given him.

3. Where did Jesus teach that we should pray?

4. Connect the Thoughts:
   Noah found it
   God's is sufficient
   come boldly to the throne of

5. In the four Gospels, we can find
   a) stories Jesus told.
   b) Jesus' family lineage.
   c) accounts of Jesus' resurrection.
   d) all of the above.

ANSWERS

1. imitators (Ephesians 5:1 NIV)
2. wisdom (James 1:5 KJV)
3. in a room with the door closed (Matthew 6:6)
4. grace (Genesis 6:8 KJV; 2 Corinthians 12:9; Hebrews 4:16)
5. d

Day 220

1. What part of Jesus' body did a sinful woman anoint with perfume and kiss during a dinner at a Pharisee's house?

2. Connect the Thoughts:
   baby Moses in his floating basket
   Jesus at Lazarus' tomb
   Peter after denying Christ

3. Match: Seventy. . .
   a) number of Solomon's wives
   b) number of half brothers of Abimelech
   c) number of Solomon's concubines

4. What was Potiphar's job?

5. To whom is the book of Acts addressed?
   a) Theophilus
   b) Barnabas
   c) Cornelius
   d) Eutychus

ANSWERS

1. His feet (Luke 7:36–38)
2. people who wept (Exodus 2:5–10; John 11:32–43; Luke 22:61–62)
3. b (Judges 9:1–2)
4. captain of the guard (Genesis 39:1)
5. a (Acts 1:1)

Day 221

1. What did Jesus do on a Sabbath day that so infuriated the Pharisees that they began plotting to kill Him?

2. Where did Jesus move to after leaving Nazareth?
   a) Capernaum
   b) Jerusalem
   c) Cana
   d) Bethany

3. Who was Jesus' first disciple?

4. John says that to all who receive Jesus, to those who believe in His name, He gives the right to become ____ of God.

5. What name for Jesus, meaning "Anointed One," did Daniel use when writing about the end times?

ANSWERS

1. healed a man (Matthew 12:9–14)
2. a (Matthew 4:13)
3. Andrew (John 1:35–41)
4. children (John 1:12 NIV)
5. Messiah (Daniel 9:25)

Day 222

1. What major prophet had a son named Shear-Jashub (NIV)?

2. When Gideon was visited by an angel, Gideon was hiding wheat from the
   a) Canaanites.
   b) Jebusites.
   c) Midianites.
   d) Electric Lights.

3. Whose wife was turned into a pillar of salt for looking back on the doomed cities of Sodom and Gomorrah?

4. Connect the Thoughts:
   son of Jephunneh
   associate of Joshua
   a positive report from Canaan

5. Match: Solomon. . .
   a) He asked God first for wealth and then for wisdom.
   b) He finished building the temple started by his father.
   c) His mother, Bathsheba, feared for her life before he was made king.

ANSWERS

1. Isaiah (Isaiah 7:3)
2. c (Judges 6:11)
3. Lot (Genesis 19:23–26)
4. Caleb (Numbers 13:6; Joshua 14:13; Numbers 13:26–30)
5. c (1 Kings 1:11–21)

Day 223

1. Right after Jesus brought the little girl back to life, He healed
    a) a little boy who had only two fish and a loaf of bread for lunch.
    b) two blind men.
    c) three blind mice.
    d) ten lepers.

2. What violent act ended the reign of the evil King Zechariah of Israel only six months after he took power?

3. Connect the Thoughts:
    a six-month party
    a hanging
    a celebration called Purim

4. According to the apostle Paul, how will the day of Jesus' return come?
    a) like a thief in the night
    b) like a mighty trumpet
    c) like a flash of lightning
    d) like an eagle swooping

5. When told that his sons had been killed and the ark of the covenant had been taken, who fell over backward and died of a broken neck?

ANSWERS

1. b (Matthew 9:24-29)
2. assassination (2 Kings 15:8–10)
3. events in the book of Esther (Esther 1:2–4; Esther 7:10; Esther 9:28)
4. a (1 Thessalonians 5:2)
5. Eli (1 Samuel 4:16–18)

Day 224

1. Complete the scripture:
   Thy word have I hid in mine heart, that I might not ___ against thee.

2. What does Romans 8:26 say that the Holy Spirit does for us?

3. According to Ecclesiastes, when should you "remember your Creator"?
   a) in the days of your youth
   b) when times of trouble come
   c) as your years increase
   d) in joy and in sorrow

4. What will the Counselor, who will live with you, teach you?

5. True or False: The God of Israel was not fooled by Jezebel's clever plan of revenge upon Naboth.

ANSWERS

1. sin (Psalm 119:11 KJV)
2. makes intercession for us
3. a (Ecclesiastes 12:1 NIV)
4. all things (John 14:26)
5. True (1 Kings 21)

Day 225

1. What businesswoman from Thyatira, a seller of purple cloth, became a Christian after hearing Paul share the gospel?

2. Connect the Thoughts:
   Joanna the wife of Chuza
   Susanna
   Mary Magdalene

3. Match: Annas. . .
   a) blessed baby Jesus in the temple.
   b) was the father-in-law of Caiaphas.
   c) accompanied Paul on his second missionary journey.

4. In his letter to the Corinthians, who were the only people Paul said he baptized?

5. Who was promised that he would not die until he saw the Messiah come?

ANSWERS

1. Lydia (Acts 16:13–15)
2. women who supported Jesus' ministry (Luke 8:1–3)
3. b (John 18:13)
4. Crispus and Gaius (1 Corinthians 1:14)
5. Simeon (Luke 2:25–26)

Day 226

1. Where did Jesus pray the night He was betrayed and arrested?

2. Aaron died at
   a) Mount Sinai.
   b) the Mount of Olives.
   c) Mount Hor.
   d) Mount Everest.

3. What major body of water is less than twenty miles from Nazareth?

4. Match: Cush. . .
   a) Egypt
   b) Ethiopia
   c) Assyria

5. What did Abraham name the place where God told him to sacrifice Isaac?

ANSWERS

1. Gethsemane (Matthew 26:36–57)
2. c (Numbers 33:38)
3. the Sea of Galilee
4. b (Isaiah 20)
5. Jehovah-jireh: The Lord Will Provide (Genesis 22:1–14)

Day 227

1. Which of the following statements did Jesus make just before He died on the cross?
    a) "It is painful."
    b) "It is unfair."
    c) "It is finished."
    d) "It is necessary."

2. Where did Jesus say that a prophet is without honor?

3. Match: Jesus' sign for the Pharisees. . .
    a) sign of catastrophic weather
    b) sign of the beheading of John the Baptist
    c) sign of Jonah

4. From what tribe did Jesus descend?

5. When a woman in Bethany poured expensive ointment on His head, Jesus
    a) said she had done something good for Him.
    b) was furious that his hairstyle was mussed.
    c) thought the gesture was a waste of money.
    d) sent her the bill for having His cloak dry cleaned.

ANSWERS

1. c (John 19:30 NIV)
2. in his hometown (Mark 6:4)
3. c (Matthew 16:1, 4 NIV)
4. Judah (Matthew 1:3–17 NIV)
5. a (Matthew 26:6–10)

Day 228

1. What tiny insect did Jesus say the hypocritical Pharisees strained out of their food, only to "swallow a camel"?

2. Connect the Thoughts:
    beautiful on the mountains
    a sinful woman's kiss for Jesus
    God's Word as a lamp

3. What did the four living creatures around the throne resemble, respectively?

4. How many golden lamp stands, each representing a church in Asia Minor, did John see in his vision of the Revelation of Christ?
    a) three
    b) five
    c) seven
    d) nine

5. What body fluid did God forbid the Israelites to eat because it holds the life of every creature?

ANSWERS

1. gnat (Matthew 23:23–24)
2. feet (Isaiah 52:7; Luke 7:36–38; Psalm 119:105)
3. lion, calf (ox NIV), man, eagle (Revelation 4:6–7)
4. c (Revelation 1:12–20)
5. blood (Leviticus 17:13–14)

Day 229

1. What idol were the Israelites worshiping with shouting and singing when Moses arrived with God's Ten Commandments?

2. Connect the Thoughts:
   adulterers
   extortioners
   drunkards

3. What grew from the ground God cursed after Adam and Eve's sin?

4. What was Jesus' command to the members of the church at Ephesus, who had "left thy first love"?
   a) weep
   b) repent
   c) pray
   d) yearn

5. Who is the man, Jesus says, who does not enter the sheep pen by the gate but climbs in some other way?

ANSWERS

1. the golden calf (Exodus 32:1–4, 17–20)
2. people who won't inherit the kingdom of God (1 Corinthians 6:9–10)
3. thorns and thistles (Genesis 3:14, 17–18)
4. b (Revelation 2:1–5 KJV)
5. a thief and a robber (John 10:1)

Day 230

1. How did Paul describe everything he had lost in his life in his efforts to gain Christ?

2. The Epistle of James tells Christians how to
   a) set up the Communion table.
   b) write a proper thank-you note.
   c) write a Sunday school curriculum for toddlers.
   d) live according to God's Word.

3. Jesus said, "The Spirit gives life," but what "counts for nothing"?

4. Complete the scripture:
   He lifted up himself, and said unto them, He that is without sin among you, let him first cast a ____ at her.

5. Whom did the five foolish virgins ask for oil for their lamps?

ANSWERS

1. rubbish, or dung (Philippians 3:7–8)
2. d
3. the flesh (John 6:63 NIV)
4. stone (John 8:7 KJV)
5. the five wise virgins (Matthew 25:1, 8)

Day 231

1. What did Samson eat from the carcass of a lion he had killed?

2. Connect the Thoughts:
   Absalom
   Samson
   Mary, sister of Martha

3. What part of the body is usually anointed?

4. Match: Lot. . .
   a) baked bread without yeast for two angels.
   b) refused to eat bread before Sodom was destroyed.
   c) baked bread to take with him out of Sodom.

5. What job was Moses doing when God spoke to him from the burning bush?

ANSWERS

1. honey (Judges 14:5–9)
2. people famed for their hair (2 Samuel 14:25–26; Judges 16:13–17; John 11:1–2)
3. the head (1 Samuel 10:1)
4. a (Genesis 19:1, 3)
5. herding sheep (Exodus 3:1–2)

Day 232

1. With what does Psalm 45 say that Jesus has been anointed?

2. Connect the Thoughts:
   the first and the last
   the light of the world
   the way, the truth, and the life

3. According to Paul, from what curse has Christ redeemed us?

4. Complete the scripture:
   Who shall ___ us from the love of Christ? shall tribulation, or distress, or persecution, or famine, or nakedness, or peril, or sword?

5. Speaking of the future, Jesus tells of wars, earthquakes, and famines that are to come. By standing firm, He says, we will gain ______.

ANSWERS

1. the "oil of joy" (Psalm 45:7 NIV)
2. "I am" statements of Jesus (Revelation 1:17–18; John 9:1–5; John 14:6)
3. curse of the law (Galatians 3:13)
4. separate (Romans 8:35 KJV)
5. life (Luke 21:10–19 NIV)

Day 233

1. What prophetess told the faithful King Josiah he would not see the disaster God was bringing on his unfaithful nation?

2. Jezebel killed Naboth so Ahab could possess his
   a) slaves.
   b) flocks.
   c) gold.
   d) vineyard.

3. What Old Testament priest, for whom a Bible book is named, worked with Nehemiah to encourage the public reading and study of scripture?

4. Connect the Thoughts:
   Don't drink wine.
   Don't cut your hair.
   Don't touch the dead.

5. Match: Hezekiah. . .
   a) He was the last king of Israel.
   b) As a sign to him, God made the shadow go forward ten steps on a sundial.
   c) God added fifteen years to his life.

ANSWERS

1. Huldah (2 Kings 22:3, 14–20)
2. d (1 Kings 21:5–15)
3. Ezra (Nehemiah 8:1–12)
4. rules for the Nazarite vow (Numbers 6:1–8)
5. c (2 Kings 20:1, 6)

Day 234

1. What annual celebration was instituted to commemorate the Jews' victory over their enemies in Queen Esther's time?

2. When Mary Magdalene first saw the risen Christ, she believed He was
   a) an angel.
   b) the gardener.
   c) a disciple playing a prank.
   d) John the Baptist.

3. Connect the Thoughts:
   the earth quakes and rocks split
   graves open and the bodies of saints come back to life
   the veil of the temple tears from top to bottom

4. What did Jesus tell the servants in Cana to do with the six stone water jars?

5. Which of the following was not one of Satan's temptations of Christ?
   a) changing stones into bread
   b) jumping off the temple
   c) worshiping the devil
   d) striking the wicked with blindness

ANSWERS

1. Purim (Esther 9:20–28)
2. b (John 20:1, 15)
3. Jesus' death (Matthew 27:50–53)
4. fill them with water (John 2:7)
5. d (Matthew 4:1–10)

Day 235

1. The apostle Paul warned Christians about being "yoked" with what?
   a) debt
   b) unbelievers
   c) sin
   d) worldly wisdom

2. Complete the scripture:
   All scripture is given by ___ of God, and is profitable for doctrine, for reproof, for correction, for instruction in righteousness.

3. According to Acts 8:39, what did the Holy Spirit do with Philip?

4. Which of the following is not on the apostle Paul's list of things to think about?
   a) whatever is true
   b) whatever is pure
   c) whatever is lovely
   d) whatever is pleasing

5. "Peace I leave with you; my peace I give you." To what peace was Jesus referring?

ANSWERS

1. b (2 Corinthians 6:14)
2. inspiration (2 Timothy 3:16 KJV)
3. caught him away
4. d (Philippians 4:8)
5. the peace conveyed by the Holy Spirit (John 14:27 NIV)

Day 236

1. What wandering preacher was imprisoned for challenging the adulterous marriage of King Herod?

2. Which of the following is *not* a hardship the apostle Paul had to endure, according to his list in 2 Corinthians 11?
   a) shipwreck
   b) beatings
   c) wild animals
   d) robbers

3. What was Matthew's job before he became a disciple of Jesus?

4. Connect the Thoughts:
   Tabitha
   helping the poor
   death and resurrection

5. True or False: When Jesus told Martha that Lazarus would rise again, she thought He meant Lazarus would rise again at the resurrection at the last day.

ANSWERS

1. John the Baptist (Mark 6:14–18)
2. c (2 Corinthians 11:23–28)
3. tax collector (Matthew 9:9)
4. Dorcas (Acts 9:36–41)
5. True (John 11:23–24)

Day 237

1. What land did the patriarch Abraham hail from?

2. Connect the Thoughts:
   Carmel
   Hermon
   Zion

3. In what city did Jesus' disciples first take the name "Christians"?

4. Match: Valley of Rephaim. . .
   a) where Abner was murdered
   b) where David twice attacked the Philistines
   c) where Saul died after battling the Philistines

5. What did Moses fear the thirsty Israelites would do to him at a dry place called Rephidim?

ANSWERS

1. Ur of the Chaldees, or Chaldeans (Genesis 15:1, 7–8)
2. mountains (1 Kings 18:19; Deuteronomy 3:8; Psalm 74:2)
3. Antioch (Acts 11:26)
4. b (2 Samuel 5:17–25)
5. stone him (Exodus 17:1–4)

Day 238

1. Why did Pilate's wife advise her husband to leave Jesus alone?
   a) She believed Isaiah's prophecies.
   b) She had seen Jesus perform miracles.
   c) She had had a bad dream.
   d) She feared a Galilean revolt.

2. As Jesus rode the donkey toward Jerusalem, what did the people throw down on the road?

3. Which of the following was not a gift the wise men brought the baby Jesus?
   a) gold
   b) diamonds
   c) frankincense
   d) myrrh

4. According to the Gospel of Mark, what did evil spirits do whenever they saw Jesus, and what did they say?

5. Match: Powers Jesus gave the disciples. . .
   a) to drive out demons and restore sight.
   b) to drive out demons and heal all diseases.
   c) to heal all diseases.

ANSWERS

1. c (Matthew 27:17–19)
2. their cloaks (Luke 19:36)
3. b (Matthew 2:1, 11)
4. Evil spirits fell down and cried out, "You are the Son of God" (Mark 3:11 NIV).
5. b (Matthew 10:1)

Day 239

1. What stinging insect did God use to drive enemy peoples out of the Promised Land?

2. Connect the Thoughts:
   Pharaoh's lost in the Red Sea
   Solomon's 1,400
   Elijah's fiery ride into heaven

3. What melting substance did the psalmist say his heart had turned to?

4. What precious metal, according to Proverbs, cannot compare to the value of wisdom?
   a) silver
   b) bronze
   c) gold
   d) iron

5. What was the sacrifice that Joseph and Mary were required to offer up for Jesus' birth?

ANSWERS

1. hornet (Joshua 24:11–12)
2. chariots (Exodus 14:28; 2 Chronicles 1:14; 2 Kings 2:11)
3. wax (Psalm 22:14)
4. c (Proverbs 16:16)
5. two turtledoves or two young pigeons (Luke 2:21–24)

Day 240

1. Connect the Thoughts:
   fig leaves
   a curse
   dust

2. Complete the scripture:
   For if you ____ men when they sin against you, your heavenly Father will also ____ you.

3. What do the Proverbs call the person who tries to add to God's Words?
   a) a liar
   b) a fool
   c) a cheat
   d) a devil

4. Who was Korah, and what happened to him?

5. Match: Jacob. . .
   a) wore Esau's best clothes with goatskin on his arms and neck.
   b) wore Esau's poorest garments with goatskin on his arms and neck.
   c) wore his own clothes and goatskin on his arms and neck.

ANSWERS

1. the sin of Adam and Eve (Genesis 3:7; Genesis 3:17; Genesis 3:19)
2. forgive, forgive (Matthew 6:14 NIV)
3. a (Proverbs 30:6)
4. He led a rebellion against Moses and Aaron and was swallowed by the earth (Numbers 16).
5. a (Genesis 27:15–16)

Day 241

1. What answer did Jesus give to an expert in the law who asked which commandment was greatest?

2. Complete the scripture:
   The effectual fervent prayer of a ____ man availeth much.

3. How did Jesus say you could recognize a tree?

4. 1 Peter was written to help
   a) raise money for new carpet in the sanctuary.
   b) Christians find other Christian businesses.
   c) suffering Christians.
   d) missionaries in South America.

5. What did the merchant do when he found the pearl of great price?

ANSWERS

1. "Love the Lord your God with all your heart and with all your soul and with all your mind" (Matthew 22:34–40 NIV).
2. righteous (James 5:16 KJV)
3. by its fruit (Matthew 12:33)
4. c
5. sold all he had and bought it (Matthew 13:45–46)

Day 242

1. Which of the following does not appear in Song of Solomon?
   a) “Your nose is like the tower of Lebanon.”
   b) “Your navel is a rounded goblet.”
   c) “Your fingers are like limbs of cedar.”
   d) “Your eyes are the pools of Heshbon.”

2. What gruesome things did Ezekiel see filling a valley?

3. Connect the Thoughts:
   Abimelech’s injury
   Jezebel’s remains
   Golgotha

4. Match: Seventeen. . .
   a) years Samson was judge of Israel
   b) shekels of silver paid to Judas for his betrayal
   c) shekels of silver paid by Jeremiah for a field

5. Which famous Bible character shared his name with a lesser-known biblical woman?
   a) Adam
   b) Daniel
   c) Moses
   d) Noah

ANSWERS

1. c (Song of Solomon 7:1–5 NIV)
2. dry bones (Ezekiel 37:1–14)
3. skulls (Judges 9:52–53; 2 Kings 9:34–37; Mark 15:22)
4. c (Jeremiah 32:9)
5. d (Numbers 27:1)

Day 243

1. When many followers decided to leave Jesus because of His controversial teachings, how many of the twelve disciples left?

2. Connect the Thoughts:
   a slave and an awl
   false teachers and things that itch
   Peter and Malchus

3. Match: Jesus' clearing of the temple occurred. . .
   a) once
   b) twice
   c) three times

4. What does John 3:17 say that God did not send Jesus to do?

5. Which of the following is not among the names of Christ in Isaiah's prophecy?
   a) Mighty God
   b) Everlasting Father
   c) Prince of Peace
   d) Hope of Man

ANSWERS

1. none (John 6:66–70)
2. ears (Deuteronomy 15:17; 2 Timothy 4:3; John 18:10)
3. b (John 2:13–17; Matthew 21:12–13)
4. condemn the world
5. d (Isaiah 9:6)

Day 244

1. What handsome son of Jacob was imprisoned after a false report from Potiphar's wife?

2. Connect the Thoughts:
   Eliphaz
   Zophar
   Elihu

3. What man, cousin of Queen Esther, served as her advisor and saved the Jews from destruction?

4. Connect the Thoughts:
   son of Saul
   warrior of Israel
   friend of David

5. Match: Jeroboam. . .
   a) He was told by a prophet that he would rule ten tribes in Israel.
   b) Solomon chose him as his successor.
   c) He built his own shrines at Jerusalem.

ANSWERS

1. Joseph (Genesis 39:2–20)
2. characters in the book of Job (Job 4:1; Job 20:1; Job 32:2)
3. Mordecai (Esther 2:7, 10:3)
4. Jonathan (1 Samuel 14:1; 1 Samuel 14:14; 1 Samuel 20:42)
5. a (1 Kings 11:29–31)

Day 245

1. Who was to die in Egyptian households on the night of Passover?

2. Elijah, a man of God, was taken to heaven
   a) in a whirlwind.
   b) in a chariot.
   c) up a stairway.
   d) by climbing a ladder.

3. What miraculous event preceded Jesus walking on water toward His disciples?

4. Connect the Thoughts:
   Stephen is stoned to death.
   Saul is converted to faith in Jesus.
   An angel releases Peter from prison.

5. What, according to 1 Corinthians, will be "swallowed up in victory" at the last trumpet?

ANSWERS

1. the firstborn (Exodus 12:11–13)
2. a (2 Kings 2:1)
3. the feeding of the five thousand (Matthew 14:13–27)
4. events in the book of Acts (Acts 7:54–60; Acts 9:1–22; Acts 12:1–11)
5. death (1 Corinthians 15:51–54 NIV)

Day 246

1. How long does the psalmist say that a thousand years are in God's sight?

2. Complete the scripture:
   Prophecy came not in old time by the ____ of man: but holy men of God spake as they were moved by the Holy Ghost.

3. What three things did Paul tell Timothy that God has given us, as opposed to a spirit of fear?

4. What type of people, according to the book of James, does God give grace to?
   a) the wise
   b) the merciful
   c) the peacemakers
   d) the humble

5. What parable illustrates how God feels about those who don't forgive others?

ANSWERS

1. as yesterday, or a day (Psalm 90:4)
2. will (2 Peter 1:21 KJV)
3. power, love, and a sound mind (2 Timothy 1:7 KJV)
4. d (James 4:6)
5. the Unforgiving Servant (Matthew 18:22–35)

Day 247

1. What woman, also known as Tabitha, was raised from the dead after Peter knelt and prayed?

2. Connect the Thoughts:
   Aceldama
   a kiss
   thirty pieces of silver

3. Match: Mary. . .
   a) sang to Elizabeth after her baby leaped in her womb.
   b) sang to Joseph after her baby leaped in her womb.
   c) sang to the angel Gabriel.

4. True or False: According to Peter, you can trust any person who claims to be a Christian.

5. After the crucifixion, who asked Pilate for Jesus' body?
   a) Simon of Cyrene
   b) Joseph of Arimathea
   c) Mary of Magdala
   d) Apollos of Alexandria

ANSWERS

1. Dorcas (Acts 9:36–41)
2. Judas Iscariot (Acts 1:16–19 KJV; Luke 22:47–48; Matthew 27:3–4)
3. a (Luke 1:39–55)
4. False (2 Peter 2:1)
5. b (Mark 15:43)

Day 248

1. What mount saw the deaths of King Saul and his sons in battle?

2. Match: Garden of Eden. . .
   a) where Adam and Eve ate from the tree of life
   b) where Adam and Eve ate from the tree of knowledge of good and evil
   c) where the tree of life was not found

3. The leaves of the tree of life in the new heaven on earth will be used for what purpose?

4. Where did Lot, apparently unwilling to move too far from the soon-to-be-destroyed Sodom, beg God's angels to let him live?
   a) Gaza
   b) Haran
   c) Ur
   d) Zoar

5. What was special about the Pool of Bethesda?

ANSWERS

1. Gilboa (1 Samuel 31:8)
2. b (Genesis 2:15–16, 3:17)
3. the healing of nations (Revelation 22:2)
4. d (Genesis 19:1–22)
5. An angel stirred up the water, and the first one in after that would be healed (John 5:2–4 KJV).

Day 249

1. What was Jesus discussing when He mentioned the name of Caesar?
   a) the fall of Rome
   b) idolatry
   c) paying taxes
   d) unjust leadership

2. Complete the scripture:
   For God did not send his Son into the world to condemn the world, but to ____ the world through him.

3. Match: Anointing of Jesus. . .
   a) done by Martha, Lazarus's sister
   b) done by pouring perfume on His head
   c) done at the home of Lazarus in Bethany

4. What did the risen Jesus say to Mary Magdalene?

5. How many apostles did Jesus personally select?
   a) two
   b) twelve
   c) fifty
   d) one thousand

ANSWERS

1. c (Luke 20:21–25)
2. save (John 3:17 NIV)
3. b (Mark 14:1–3)
4. "Why are you crying?" (John 20:11–15 NIV)
5. b (Luke 6:13)

Day 250

1. What valuable red stones, according to Proverbs, are worth less than either wisdom or a good wife?

2. Connect the Thoughts:
   the earth, to God
   enemies, to Christ
   a place of dishonor, to the poor

3. What food was to be stored in the ark of the covenant?

4. What sign protected Israelite homes in Egypt from the plague on the firstborn?
   a) a candle in the window
   b) bread in the oven
   c) a goat in the yard
   d) blood on the doorposts

5. What beast of burden was forbidden as food to the Israelites?

ANSWERS

1. rubies (Proverbs 8:11, 31:10)
2. footstools (Isaiah 66:1; Matthew 22:41–45; James 2:3)
3. pot of manna (Exodus 16:32–34)
4. d (Exodus 12:23)
5. camel (Leviticus 11:4)

Day 251

1. According to James, what is "friendship with the world"?
   a) a grievous sin
   b) hatred toward God
   c) a poisonous viper
   d) the foolishness of man

2. What beautiful wife of Uriah was improperly taken—and made pregnant—by a lustful King David?

3. True or False: Both John and Jude condemn false teachers in their letters.

4. Which of the following is not listed as part of King Nebuchadnezzar's punishment for pride?
   a) He ate grass like cattle.
   b) His hair grew like a bird's feathers.
   c) His nails grew like a bird's claws.
   d) He slept in a wet cave.

5. Who rebuked Sanballat when his army ridiculed the people of the Lord?

ANSWERS

1. b (James 4:4 NIV)
2. Bathsheba (2 Samuel 11:2–5)
3. True
4. d (Daniel 4:33)
5. Nehemiah (Nehemiah 6)

Day 252

1. What two-part answer did Jesus give to trouble-making Pharisees who asked Him whether they should pay taxes to Caesar?

2. Who, according to Paul, is to have first responsibility for caring for a widow in the church?
   a) the widow herself
   b) her children and other relatives
   c) the church
   d) the government

3. Connect the Thoughts:
   food
   drink
   clothing

4. What did Jesus say we should do to those who persecute us?

5. True or False: Anyone who is persecuted for any reason will be blessed.

ANSWERS

1. "Give to Caesar what is Caesar's and to God what is God's" (Mark 12:13–17 NIV).
2. b (1 Timothy 5:4)
3. things Jesus said not to worry about (Matthew 6:31–32)
4. pray for them (Matthew 5:44)
5. False (Matthew 5:10)

Day 253

1. According to the apostle Paul, in trials and hardships Christians are "more than" what?
   a) conquerors
   b) angels
   c) warriors
   d) kings

2. What role did Boaz play by marrying Ruth and purchasing the property of her former in-laws?

3. In addition to Genesis, what other book of the Bible starts, "In the beginning"?
   a) Job
   b) Daniel
   c) Luke
   d) John

4. Connect the Thoughts:
   graven
   man made in God's
   Christ, of the invisible God

5. Sanballat and Tobiah are villains in what biblical book?
   a) Esther
   b) Nehemiah
   c) Obadiah
   d) Daniel

ANSWERS

1. a (Romans 8:37)
2. kinsman-redeemer (Ruth 3:7–13; 4:9–10, 13–14 NIV)
3. d (John 1:1)
4. image (Exodus 20:4 KJV; Genesis 1:26; Colossians 1:15)
5. b (Nehemiah 6:1–2)

Day 254

1. When Mary Magdalene heard Jesus say her name following His resurrection, how did she address Him?

2. Complete this quotation of Jesus:
“Then you will know the truth, . . .
    a) “and the truth will set you free.”
    b) “and you will be wise.”
    c) “and many will accept your teaching.”
    d) “and you will enjoy prosperity.”

3. Where has the Lord Jesus been since the Ascension, according to Mark’s Gospel?

4. Connect the Thoughts:
    Chief Shepherd
    Lamb of God
    Lion of the tribe of Judah

5. What did the disciples in the boat say to Jesus when the storm had passed?

ANSWERS

1. “Rabboni!” (John 20:16 NIV)
2. a (John 8:32 NIV)
3. in heaven, sitting at the right hand of God (Mark 16:19)
4. titles of Jesus Christ (1 Peter 5:1–4; John 1:29; Revelation 5:5)
5. “Truly you are the Son of God” (Matthew 14:22–33 NIV).

Day 255

1. What did the elderly Sarah do when she was told she would give birth to Isaac?

2. After Esther became queen, Mordecai found favor by
   a) doubling the grapes produced by the king's vineyards.
   b) foiling an assassination attempt on a provincial governor.
   c) foiling an assassination attempt on the king.
   d) storing enough grain to take the provinces through a seven-year famine.

3. What beautiful daughter of David was mistreated by her stepbrother Amnon—who paid for that sin with his life?

4. Connect the Thoughts:
   Ham
   Japheth
   Shem

5. Match: Rehoboam. . .
   a) He followed in David's footsteps by worshiping the Lord.
   b) He sold all the treasures of the temple to Jeroboam.
   c) He ruled over a divided kingdom.

ANSWERS

1. laugh (Genesis 18:10–12)
2. c (Esther 2:21–23)
3. Tamar (2 Samuel 13:1–14, 28–29)
4. sons of Noah (Genesis 6:10)
5. c (1 Kings 12:17)

Day 256

1. According to Jude, what did the devil and Michael the archangel fight over?
   a) the conversion of Saul
   b) the temptation of Jesus
   c) the mind of Judas Iscariot
   d) the body of Moses

2. What sound from heaven accompanied God's work at Pentecost?

3. Connect the Thoughts:
   daytime darkness
   mocking soldiers
   two thieves

4. Match: Jesus' crucifixion. . .
   a) The sun stopped in the middle of the sky.
   b) The temple curtain was torn in two from top to bottom.
   c) The Red Sea was turned to blood.

5. What does the voice of the "living creature" resemble when the Lamb breaks the first seal on the seven-sealed book of Revelation?

ANSWERS

1. d (Jude 9)
2. a violent, or mighty, wind (Acts 2:1–4)
3. the crucifixion of Jesus (Mark 15:16–33)
4. b (Mark 15:16–39)
5. thunder (Revelation 5:1, 6:1 NIV)

Day 257

1. Who knows the Father, according to Jesus in Luke's Gospel?

2. According to Jesus, what would not fall to the ground apart from God's will?
   a) a sparrow
   b) a rain drop
   c) a leaf
   d) brimstone

3. How do those who do not have God's Spirit consider the things of God?

4. Complete the scripture:
   Without faith it is impossible to ___ him: for he that cometh to God must believe that he is, and that he is a rewarder of them that diligently seek him.

5. In Isaiah 63:9, whom does Isaiah say God used to save His people?

ANSWERS

1. "the Son and those to whom the Son chooses to reveal him" (Luke 10:22 NIV)
2. a (Matthew 10:29)
3. as foolishness (1 Corinthians 2:14)
4. please (Hebrews 11:6 KJV)
5. the angel of His presence

Day 258

1. What servant girl, in her excitement at learning Peter was out of prison and at the door, left him knocking while she ran to tell the other disciples?

2. Connect the Thoughts:
   cousin of Barnabas
   profitable to Paul's ministry
   author of a Gospel

3. Match: Simeon. . .
   a) sang a song of joy with Anna upon leaving the temple.
   b) sang praises to God while holding the baby Jesus.
   c) sang praises upon entering the temple the day he saw the baby Jesus.

4. During Stephen's trial, he looked like
   a) a guilty prisoner.
   b) a bored young man.
   c) an angel.
   d) an angry young man.

5. True or False: Stephen asked God to forgive the people who punished him.

ANSWERS

1. Rhoda (Acts 12:12–16)
2. Mark (Colossians 4:10 NIV; 2 Timothy 4:11)
3. b (Luke 2:27–32)
4. c (Acts 6:15)
5. True (Acts 7:59–60)

Day 259

1. Where does "the river of the water of life" in the new Jerusalem originate?

2. Connect the Thoughts:
   Horeb
   Gilboa
   Gerizim

3. How many cities were allotted to the priests in the Promised Land?

4. Which of the following does the Bible not list as a gate in the wall of Jerusalem?
   a) Valley Gate
   b) Dung Gate
   c) Lion Gate
   d) Fountain Gate

5. What region separated Judea from Galilee?

ANSWERS

1. the throne of God (Revelation 22:1–2 NIV)
2. mountains (Exodus 33:6; 2 Samuel 1:6; Judges 9:7)
3. thirteen (Joshua 21:1–2, 19)
4. c (Nehemiah 3:13–15)
5. Samaria

Day 260

1. When a soldier pierced Jesus' side with a spear following His death, what flowed out of Jesus?

2. Jesus healed Peter's mother-in-law of
   a) leprosy.
   b) demon possession.
   c) blindness.
   d) a fever.

3. What is the first thing Jesus says to His disciples—in fact, He says it twice—when they are all together following His resurrection?

4. What led the wise men to the baby Jesus?
   a) a billboard
   b) a dove
   c) a cloud
   d) a star

5. What *S* word completes this sentence? "For God did not appoint us to suffer wrath but to receive ____ through our Lord Jesus Christ."

ANSWERS

1. blood and water (John 19:33–34)
2. d (Mark 1:30–31)
3. "Peace be with you!" (John 20:19–21 NIV)
4. d (Matthew 2:1–9)
5. salvation (1 Thessalonians 5:9 NIV)

Day 261

1. According to Jeremiah, where does one go to find balm?
    a) Babylon
    b) Jerusalem
    c) Gilead
    d) Beersheba

2. What did the psalmist say God's words, or promises, are sweeter than?

3. Connect the Thoughts:
    complaining, hungry Israelites
    dew
    bread from heaven

4. What did Jeroboam place in Dan and Bethel for the people to worship?

5. Match: Hyssop. . .
    a) Babylonian fortress
    b) Egyptian song
    c) plant with stalks

ANSWERS

1. c (Jeremiah 8:22)
2. honey (Psalm 119:103)
3. manna (Exodus 16:1–15)
4. two golden calves (1 Kings 12:28–32)
5. c (John 19:29)

Day 262

1. Who did Adam blame when God confronted him about eating the forbidden fruit?

2. Which of these churches of Asia Minor did Jesus threaten to spit from his mouth?
   a) Ephesus
   b) Smyrna
   c) Philadelphia
   d) Laodicea

3. What king was condemned for acting as a priest?

4. Match: Jonah. . .
   a) was on his way to Nineveh when a storm arose.
   b) proclaimed that Nineveh would be overturned in seven days.
   c) was thrown overboard, and the sea became calm.

5. After discovering their nakedness, how did Adam and Eve clothe themselves?

ANSWERS

1. the woman, Eve (Genesis 3:11–12)
2. d (Revelation 3:14–16)
3. Saul (1 Samuel 13:8–14)
4. c (Jonah 1:15)
5. They sewed themselves aprons made of fig leaves (Genesis 3:6–7).

Day 263

1. What did Jesus say servants should be doing when their master, returning from a wedding banquet, knocked on the door?

2. Complete the scripture:
"If anyone loves me," Jesus said, "he will obey my ___."

3. What occupation did Paul say the law held in regard to us?

4. Complete the scripture:
When Jesus had lifted up himself, and saw none but the woman, he said unto her, Woman, where are those thine accusers? hath no man condemned thee? She said, No man, Lord. And Jesus said unto her, Neither do I condemn thee: go, and ___ ___ ___.

5. What parable included the concept of "eat, drink, and be merry"?

ANSWERS

1. watching (Luke 12:35–38)
2. teaching (John 14:23 NIV)
3. schoolmaster (tutor) (Galatians 3:24 KJV)
4. sin no more (John 8:10–11 KJV)
5. the rich fool (Luke 12:16–21)

Day 264

1. According to the Proverbs, what has the power of life and death?
   a) the tongue
   b) the king
   c) the rich
   d) the heart

2. What kind of kiss did the apostle Paul tell the Corinthians to greet each other with?

3. Connect the Thoughts:
   a sin of David
   a duty of Moses
   a command of Caesar Augustus

4. What arrow-carrying case did the psalmist liken to a man with many sons?

5. Match: Kinsman-redeemer. . .
   a) close relative who took responsibility for family
   b) brother of widow's husband
   c) nephew of widow's husband

ANSWERS

1. a (Proverbs 18:21)
2. holy (1 Corinthians 16:20; 2 Corinthians 13:12)
3. censuses (1 Chronicles 21:1; Numbers 26:1–2; Luke 2:1)
4. quiver (Psalm 127:4–5)
5. a (Ruth 2:20 NIV)

Day 265

1. At what event did Jesus' face shine like the sun and His clothes become as white as the light?

2. Which of the following disciples was not with Jesus when He was arrested at Gethsemane?
   a) Andrew
   b) Peter
   c) James
   d) John

3. What, according to the book of Hebrews, did Jesus endure "for the joy that was set before him"?

4. What word completes Jesus' saying, "Many are called, but few are ____"?

5. What do we usually call the prayer Jesus taught His disciples?

ANSWERS

1. the Transfiguration (Matthew 17:2)
2. a (Mark 14:32–33)
3. the cross (Hebrews 12:2 KJV)
4. chosen (Matthew 22:14 KJV)
5. the Lord's Prayer (Matthew 6:9–13)

Day 266

1. What king unwittingly signed a decree that caused his friend, Daniel, to be thrown into a den of lions?

2. Connect the Thoughts:
   Sarai
   Rachel
   the wife of Manoah

3. What was the name of Ruth's first husband, who died?

4. Match: Josiah. . .
   a) He was seven years old when he began his reign.
   b) He destroyed all forms of idol worship except Asherah poles.
   c) He renewed Judah's covenant with God.

5. Who was Methuselah's father?

ANSWERS

1. Darius (Daniel 6:1–16)
2. barren women (Genesis 11:30; Genesis 29:31; Judges 13:2)
3. Mahlon (Ruth 4:10)
4. c (2 Kings 22:1, 23: 1–3)
5. Enoch (Genesis 5:22)

Day 267

1. When Jesus entered Jerusalem riding on a donkey, people shouted, "Blessed is he who comes in the name of the Lord!" They also used what one Hebrew word that means "save"?

2. Connect the Thoughts:
   Unleavened Bread
   Weeks
   Tabernacles

3. When John sees the new Jerusalem coming down out of heaven, he compares the city to what?

4. Match: Jesus' crucifixion. . .
   a) Jesus' legs were broken by soldiers.
   b) Only water flowed from His pierced side.
   c) It occurred the day before the Sabbath.

5. The Feast of Unleavened Bread was first established in what Old Testament book?

ANSWERS

1. "Hosanna!" (Mark 11:9 NIV)
2. feasts of Israel (Deuteronomy 16:16)
3. a bride beautifully dressed for her husband (Revelation 21:2 NIV)
4. c (John 19:31)
5. Exodus (Exodus 12:17)

Day 268

1. Who called God "the One who sees"?

2. Connect the Thoughts:

    a rainbow
    four beasts
    twenty-four elders

3. What did Jesus do to the disciples, after His resurrection, before He gave them His Spirit?

4. Complete the scripture:
   Behold, what manner of love the Father hath bestowed upon us, that we should be ____ the sons of God.

5. To what protective cover did King David, fleeing his treasonous son Absalom, compare God?
    a) helmet
    b) wall
    c) hedge
    d) shield

ANSWERS

1. Hagar (Genesis 16:8, 13 NIV)
2. things that surround God's throne in heaven (Revelation 4:1–8)
3. He breathed on them (John 20:21–22)
4. called (1 John 3:1 KJV)
5. d (Psalm 3:3)

Day 269

1. At the time of Stephen's death, Saul was
    a) writing letters to the Christian churches.
    b) raising money for the Young Men's Mission Society at his church.
    c) putting Christians in prison.
    d) free on parole from prison.

2. What woman complained when her sister Mary chose to spend time with the visiting Jesus rather than help her with housework?

3. Who is quoted in the Bible as saying, "We ought to obey God rather than men"?
    a) Abraham
    b) Noah
    c) Jonah
    d) Peter

4. Match: Barnabas. . .
    a) brought Saul from Tarsus to Antioch.
    b) was put in prison with Peter in Jerusalem.
    c) predicted a severe famine throughout the Roman world.

5. What tribe must John the Baptist have come from?

ANSWERS

1. c (Acts 8:3)
2. Martha (Luke 10:38–42)
3. d (Acts 5:29 KJV)
4. a (Acts 11:25–26)
5. Levi, since his father was a priest (Luke 1:5)

Day 270

1. What city's name appears in the name of its "biggest" resident—Goliath?

2. Connect the Thoughts:
   a letter from the apostle Paul
   a riot over the goddess Diana
   a first love forsaken

3. Where did Jesus encounter a woman at a well?

4. Match: Garden of Gethsemane. . .
   a) All twelve disciples accompanied Jesus.
   b) All of the disciples came except Judas Iscariot.
   c) Jesus found the disciples sleeping three times.

5. In the city described in Revelation 21, are the twelve gates or the twelve foundations named for the tribes?

ANSWERS

1. Gath (1 Samuel 17:4)
2. Ephesus (Ephesians 1:1; Acts 19:23–41; Revelation 2:1–7)
3. Samaria (John 4)
4. c (Mark 14:32, 41)
5. gates (Revelation 21:12)

Day 271

1. Match: Capernaum. . .
   a) where the Shunammite woman's child was restored to life
   b) where Paul and Apollos preached
   c) where Jesus began His public ministry

2. Just prior to feeding the five thousand, where had Jesus been?

3. Connect the Thoughts:
   spitting
   striking
   a crown of thorns

4. Even though Stephen was unjustly accused of a crime and paid for it with his life, he asked God to forgive his enemies. Whose example was Stephen following?

5. Complete the scripture:
   Let the word of Christ dwell in you ___.

ANSWERS

1. c (Matthew 4:12–17)
2. He had withdrawn in a boat to a solitary place (Matthew 14:13–21).
3. the Roman soldiers' mocking of Jesus (Matthew 27:27–31)
4. Stephen was following Jesus' example of asking God to forgive those who crucified Him (Acts 7:60; Luke 23:34).
5. richly (Colossians 3:16 KJV)

Day 272

1. What kind of animal did God tell the Israelites to slaughter and eat during the Passover?

2. Samson killed a lion with
   a) his bare hands.
   b) a slingshot.
   c) a sword.
   d) the jaw of a jackass.

3. Connect the Thoughts:
   earrings
   an idol
   ground to powder

4. What happened to the scapegoat after it was presented to the Lord?

5. Match: Ephod. . .
   a) dry measure
   b) god of the Hittites
   c) linen garment worn by priests

ANSWERS

1. a lamb (Exodus 12:3–6)
2. a (Judges 14:5–6)
3. the golden calf (Exodus 32:2–20)
4. It was released to the wilderness (Leviticus 16:7–10, 21–22).
5. c (Exodus 39:1–7)

Day 273

1. What does the Bible say turned Solomon's heart from God during the latter years of his life?
    a) extreme wealth
    b) foreign wives
    c) military successes
    d) human philosophy

2. Why did Joshua lose the first battle against Ai?

3. Match: Joab. . .
    a) killed Absalom against David's orders.
    b) plotted with Absalom against David.
    c) refused to send Uriah to the front lines of battle.

4. Complete the scripture:
    What shall we say, then? Shall we go on ____ so that grace may increase? By no means!

5. True or False: It is okay to show favoritism.

ANSWERS

1. b (1 Kings 11:1–4)
2. Because Israel had sinned (Joshua 7:2–11).
3. a (2 Samuel 18:1–16)
4. sinning (Romans 6:1–2 NIV)
5. False (James 2:9)

Day 274

1. What two things, according to Jesus, destroy treasures on earth?

2. What does Galatians 6:2 say we are to do to fulfill the law of Christ?

3. True or False: In Ephesians, Paul reminds us that we all worship one God because all other gods are false.

4. Jesus told His disciples that they must be as innocent as doves and as shrewd as what creatures?

5. According to Psalm 1:1–2, what man does God bless?

ANSWERS

1. moth and rust (Matthew 6:19)
2. bear one another's burdens
3. True (Ephesians 4:6)
4. snakes or serpents (Matthew 10:16)
5. one whose delight is in the law of the Lord

Day 275

1. When Paul refers to saints, he means
   a) only those who have died.
   b) people who have helped him in the past.
   c) the New Orleans NFL football team.
   d) Christians.

2. What supernatural source of nighttime light led the Israelites on their journey out of Egypt?

3. Connect the Thoughts:
   a sea
   seasoning for speech
   Lot's wife

4. What metal tool miraculously floated for the prophet Elisha?

5. Match: Nephilim. . .
   a) Cain's descendants
   b) Naphtali's descendants
   c) giants

ANSWERS

1. d (Romans 1:7)
2. a pillar of fire (Exodus 13:18–22)
3. salt (Genesis 14:3; Colossians 4:6; Genesis 19:23–26)
4. ax (2 Kings 6:1–7)
5. c (Genesis 6:4; Numbers 13:33)

Day 276

1. Connect the Thoughts:
   James
   Simon
   Judas

2. As the blood sacrifice for our sins, Jesus the Redeemer is often likened to what Old Testament offering?

3. Complete the scripture:
   Speaking of Jesus, the apostle John writes, "In him was life, and that life was the __ of men."

4. What word did Jesus use to describe the workers compared to the "plentiful" harvest of souls?

5. Jesus said, "Behold, I send you forth as sheep in the midst of wolves: be ye therefore wise as serpents, and harmless as doves." This means
   a) God will protect you from every enemy.
   b) don't let anything get in your way.
   c) don't dress as a sheep for a costume party.
   d) be wise, but do not hurt anyone.

ANSWERS

1. brothers of Jesus (Matthew 13:53–55)
2. a lamb (Revelation 5:6–9)
3. light (John 1:4 NIV)
4. few (Luke 10:2 NIV)
5. d (Matthew 10:16 KJV)

Day 277

1. What "weeping prophet" was imprisoned in a dungeon on false charges of deserting to the enemy?

2. What Old Testament character literally wrestled with God?
   a) Noah
   b) Jacob
   c) Enoch
   d) David

3. True or False: Joseph gained favor with Pharaoh by interpreting his dreams.

4. Connect the Thoughts:
   a valley full of bones
   a man with a measuring reed
   a wheel inside a wheel

5. Match: Adonijah. . .
   a) He became king without telling his father, David.
   b) Solomon killed him while he was sleeping.
   c) He had his future wife's husband killed in battle.

ANSWERS

1. Jeremiah (Jeremiah 37:12–16)
2. b (Genesis 32:22–30)
3. True (Genesis 41:14–44)
4. visions of Ezekiel (Ezekiel 37:1; Ezekiel 40:5; Ezekiel 1:15–16)
5. a (1 Kings 1:11)

Day 278

1. How many basketfuls of broken pieces of food were left over, after the feeding of the five thousand?

2. On the day of Jezebel's death, she was
   a) thrown out of a window.
   b) trod by horses.
   c) eaten by dogs until nothing remained but her skull, palms, and feet.
   d) all of the above.

3. Match: Jesus' resurrection. . .
   a) Soldiers refused the money of the chief priests to say they moved His body.
   b) An angel told the women to meet Jesus in Galilee.
   c) Jesus appeared first to His disciples.

4. True or False: If an Israelite were away from home, it was permissible for that person to eat leavened bread during the Feast of Unleavened Bread.

5. When Joseph first discovered Mary's pregnancy, he
   a) started to cry.
   b) was full of joy.
   c) suggested Mary should be stoned.
   d) planned to break off the engagement quietly.

ANSWERS

1. twelve basketfuls (Matthew 14:20–21)
2. d (2 Kings 9:30–37)
3. b (Matthew 28:5–7)
4. False (Exodus 12:20)
5. d (Matthew 1:19)

Day 279

1. Today, God speaks to us
   a) through a megaphone.
   b) by playing recordings backwards.
   c) by appearing in a burning bush.
   d) through His Son, Jesus.

2. What should we not do to the Holy Spirit?

3. Complete the scripture:
   If we ask any thing according to his ____, he heareth us.

4. When will God wipe away all tears and eliminate death?

5. When the Lord heard Daniel's request not to eat the king's food, what did the Lord grant Daniel?
   a) great wealth
   b) favor and compassion
   c) wisdom
   d) honor and fame

ANSWERS

1. d (Hebrews 1:1–2)
2. quench Him (1 Thessalonians 5:19)
3. will (1 John 5:14 KJV)
4. in the new heaven and new earth (Revelation 21:1, 4)
5. b (Daniel 1:8–9)

Day 280

1. What man was chosen by lot to be the twelfth disciple in place of the departed Judas Iscariot?

2. Connect the Thoughts:
   glorified God at the Crucifixion
   Cornelius of the Italian band
   Jesus healed his servant

3. What leprous army commander, told to wash in the Jordan for healing, preferred to wash in the Abana or Pharpar rivers of his homeland?

4. Match: Timothy. . .
   a) accompanied Paul on his first missionary journey.
   b) was circumcised by Paul because his father was Greek.
   c) had a sharp disagreement with Paul and ministered with Barnabas.

5. What silversmith made shrines of the goddess Diana in Ephesus?

ANSWERS

1. Matthias (Acts 1:23–26)
2. centurions (Luke 23:46–47; Acts 10:1; Matthew 8:5–13)
3. Naaman (2 Kings 5:1, 10–14)
4. b (Acts 16:1–3)
5. Demetrius (Acts 19:24)

Day 281

1. What mountain chain was the final stopping point for Noah's ark?

2. Connect the Thoughts:
   the murdered Naboth
   Jesus' parable of hired workers
   Noah's drunkenness

3. John the Baptist preached in the wilderness located in ____.

4. Match: Merom. . .
   a) where Moses struck the rock for water
   b) where Haggai received God's prophecy
   c) where the northern kings camped to attack Israel

5. What was the first tribe to set foot in the Promised Land?

ANSWERS

1. Ararat (Genesis 8:1–4)
2. vineyards (1 Kings 21:15–16; Matthew 20:1–16; Genesis 9:20–21)
3. Judea (Matthew 3:1)
4. c (Joshua 11:1–5)
5. Levi (Joshua 3:1–6)

Day 282

1. To him who overcomes, Jesus said He would give some "hidden manna" and what else?

2. Complete Jesus' sentence: "For as lightning that comes from the east is visible even in the west, so will be the coming of the ____ ____ ____."

3. True or False: Peter says we are more like Jesus when we give up worldly things.

4. What did Jesus once say a worker was worthy of?

5. We should be watchful because
   a) someone might steal our treasures.
   b) we don't know when Jesus will return.
   c) we might have forgotten to turn on our security systems.
   d) our watchdog is at the vet.

ANSWERS

1. a white stone (Revelation 2:17)
2. Son of Man (Matthew 24:27 NIV)
3. True (2 Peter 1:3–4)
4. his wages, or hire (Luke 10:1–2, 7)
5. b (Matthew 24:42)

Day 283

1. What metal did Moses use to fashion a snake image that healed Israelites bitten by venomous serpents?

2. Connect the Thoughts:
   the dream of Pharaoh's baker
   leftovers at the feeding of the five thousand
   the apostle Paul's escape from Damascus

3. What animal did Goliath compare himself to when he saw David approaching him?

4. What destroyed the golden-headed statue in King Nebuchadnezzar's dream?
   a) a violent whirlwind
   b) a flood of the Euphrates River
   c) a mighty angel of God
   d) a rock not cut by human hands

5. What are the colors of the four horses mentioned in Revelation 6?

ANSWERS

1. bronze, or brass (Numbers 21:4–9)
2. baskets (Genesis 40:16–17; Matthew 14:13–21; 2 Corinthians 11:30–33)
3. dog (1 Samuel 17:4, 43)
4. d (Daniel 2:32–34)
5. white, fiery red, black, pale

Day 284

1. Complete the scripture:
   When you sin against your brothers in this way and wound their weak ____, you sin against Christ.

2. What kind of god had the people of Athens built an altar to—prompting the apostle Paul to share the true God with them?

3. According to the book of Romans, who has sinned and fallen short of God's glory?
   a) Jews
   b) Gentiles
   c) pagans
   d) all

4. Who said, "I have sinned, for I have betrayed innocent blood."

5. Match: Achan. . .
   a) was the father of Othniel, who married Acsah.
   b) hid plunder from battles in his tent.
   c) was exiled to Babylon.

ANSWERS

1. conscience (1 Corinthians 8:12 NIV)
2. unknown (Acts 17:22–23)
3. d (Romans 3:23)
4. Judas Iscariot (Matthew 27:3–4 NIV)
5. b (Joshua 7:20–21)

Day 285

1. What feeling toward money is "a root of all kinds of evil"?

2. Which of the following is not one of the Ten Commandments?
   a) You shall not murder.
   b) You shall not steal.
   c) Honor your father and mother.
   d) You shall not gossip.

3. In the parable of the good samaritan, what two men pass by the wounded man without stopping to help him?

4. According to the apostle Paul, "it is better to marry than to" what?
   a) taste the riches of this world
   b) speak in tongues
   c) burn with passion
   d) serve the Lord alone

5. According to Peter, how are we to resist our adversary the devil?

ANSWERS

1. love (1 Timothy 6:10 NIV)
2. d (Exodus 20:3–17)
3. a priest and a Levite (Luke 10:31–32)
4. c (1 Corinthians 7:9)
5. by standing steadfast in the faith (1 Peter 5:8–9)

Day 286

1. Which of the following is not a biblical nationality?
   a) Canaanite
   b) Perizzite
   c) Jebusite
   d) Woolite

2. What two cloth items, after being touched by the apostle Paul, were used to heal the sick and drive out demons?

3. Connect the Thoughts:
   Elisha
   the eagle
   forbidden for priests

4. Where did Moses obtain water for the quarreling Israelites at a dry place called Kadesh?

5. Match: Song of the Lamb. . .
   a) sung before the seventh trumpet sounded
   b) sung by the two witnesses in Jerusalem
   c) sung before the final seven bowl judgments

ANSWERS

1. d
2. handkerchiefs and aprons (Acts 19:11–12)
3. baldness (2 Kings 2:22–23; Micah 1:16; Leviticus 21:1–5)
4. from a rock (Numbers 20:1–11)
5. c (Revelation 15:2–4, 16:1–17)

Day 287

1. What *Y* word does Jesus use in the following passage? "Come to me, all you who are weary and burdened . . . for my ____ is easy and my burden is light."

2. Jesus said,"I am the vine; you are the" what?
   a) grapes
   b) leaves
   c) branches
   d) thorns

3. True or False: Jesus is the chief cornerstone.

4. To whom did Jesus say, "You would have no power over me if it were not given to you from above"?

5. If we accept Jesus, we will find
   a) a way to make good grades in school.
   b) mercy and grace.
   c) a lot of money.
   d) many friends.

ANSWERS

1. yoke (Matthew 11:28, 30 NIV)
2. c (John 15:5 NIV)
3. True (1 Peter 2:6–7)
4. Pontius Pilate (John 19:10–11 NIV)
5. b (Hebrews 4:16)

Day 288

1. Joseph's brothers hated him even more after Joseph dreamed that
   a) there would be a famine.
   b) his brothers would serve Joseph.
   c) his brothers would invent the paper clip.
   d) Joseph would be the lead singer of the Partridge Family.

2. What woman helped Deborah earn a complete military victory by driving a tent peg through the head of the sleeping enemy commander, Sisera?

3. Connect the Thoughts:
   an uncircumcised Philistine
   a stone in a sling
   a severed head

4. By what other name was Gideon known?

5. Match: Zerubbabel. . .
   a) led the second group of exiles from Babylon to Jerusalem.
   b) rebuilt the temple in Jerusalem.
   c) was one of Governor Darius's chief officials.

ANSWERS

1. b (Genesis 37:5–8)
2. Jael (Judges 4:17–21)
3. Goliath (1 Samuel 17:3–51)
4. Jerubbaal (Judges 7:1)
5. b (Ezra 5:2, 6:14)

Day 289

1. Mary gave birth to Jesus in
   a) the finest medical facility available, since Jesus is the Messiah.
   b) her home.
   c) a stable, because there was no room for them at the inn.
   d) a palace.

2. For the celebration of which feast did Jesus arrive in Jerusalem secretly, instead of publicly as His earthly brothers wished?

3. Match: Judas Iscariot's betrayal. . .
   a) Soldiers came to arrest Jesus unarmed.
   b) Soldiers attacked Jesus with clubs.
   c) Judas identified Jesus with the word "Rabbi," or "Master," and a kiss.

4. Who had a vision of heaven as he was being martyred for his strong preaching?
   a) Stephen
   b) Matthias
   c) Paul
   d) Timothy

5. Who suggested that Elisha could cure Naaman?

ANSWERS

1. c (Luke 2:4–7)
2. Feast of the Tabernacles (John 7:2, 10)
3. c (Mark 14:43–45)
4. a (Acts 7:54–60)
5. a servant girl (2 Kings 5:2–3)

Day 290

1. When God told Abram to leave Ur, what did He promise him?

2. Connect the Thoughts:
   Nissi
   Shalom
   Jireh

3. On what occasion did God "repent," or regret something He had done?

4. Complete the scripture:
   Ye are of God, little children, and have overcome them: because ___ is he that is in you, than he that is in the world.

5. How long does the writer of Psalm 45 say God's throne will last?

ANSWERS

1. that He would make Abram's name great and through him all nations would be blessed (Genesis 12:1–3)
2. words connected with "Jehovah" (Exodus 17:15 KJV; Judges 6:24 KJV; Genesis 22:14 KJV)
3. when He saw that every thought of man was evil continually (Genesis 6:5–8)
4. greater (1 John 4:4 KJV)
5. for ever and ever (Psalm 45:6 KJV)

Day 291

1. Who is the only witch mentioned in the Bible?

2. What fellow government official—formerly an enemy—became Pontius Pilate's friend during Jesus' trial?

3. Match: Shepherds. . .
   a) sang for joy upon seeing angels outside Bethlehem.
   b) sang to their sheep after seeing baby Jesus.
   c) were sung to by angels outside Bethlehem.

4. What famous relative of Jesus did Isaiah and Malachi both foretell?

5. Why were the seven chosen in Acts 6?

ANSWERS

1. witch of Endor (1 Samuel 28:7–8)
2. Herod (Luke 23:5–12)
3. c (Luke 2:8–14)
4. John the Baptist (Isaiah 40:3; Malachi 3:1)
5. to make sure the Greek widows were provided for (Acts 6:1–3)

Day 292

1. What city, whose name means "house of God," was the site of an altar built by Jacob?

2. Miriam was buried in
    a) Egypt.
    b) Kadesh.
    c) Bethlehem.
    d) Canaan.

3. How long was the ark of the covenant kept in Kirjath-jearim?

4. Match: Carmel. . .
    a) where Elijah ascended on a chariot of fire
    b) where Ahab assembled the prophets of Baal
    c) where Elijah hid from Jezebel

5. Complete the scripture:
Jacob said to Rebekah his mother, "But my brother ____ is a hairy man, and I'm a man with ____ skin."

ANSWERS

1. Bethel (Genesis 35:1)
2. b (Numbers 20:1)
3. twenty years (1 Samuel 7:2)
4. b (1 Kings 18:19–20)
5. Esau, smooth (Genesis 27:11 NIV)

Day 293

1. When Paul writes that Jesus is "head of the body," what body is that?

2. According to Jesus, "the greatest among you will be. . ."
   a) "the winner of souls."
   b) "the worker of miracles."
   c) "your teacher."
   d) "your servant."

3. When Jesus prophesied about His death, which minor prophet did He say was a sign?

4. Complete the scripture:
   I delivered unto you first of all that which I also received, how that Christ died for our sins according to the ___.

5. What did the centurion say when the earth quaked at Jesus' crucifixion?

ANSWERS

1. the church (Colossians 1:18)
2. d (Matthew 23:11 NIV)
3. Jonah, or Jonas (Matthew 12:39–40)
4. scriptures (1 Corinthians 15:3 KJV)
5. "Truly this was the Son of God" (Matthew 27:54 KJV).

Day 294

1. What baking product was banned from Israelite homes for an entire week during the Passover celebration?

2. Connect the Thoughts:
   Uzzah's death
   the Ten Commandments
   gold plating

3. What did the four beasts represent in Daniel's vision?

4. What kind of bug does Proverbs say should be an example for lazy people?
   a) jitterbug
   b) moth
   c) grasshopper
   d) ant

5. What part of the city wall of the new Jerusalem is decorated with precious stones?

ANSWERS

1. yeast, or leaven (Exodus 12:19, 43)
2. the ark of the covenant (2 Samuel 6:6–7; Deuteronomy 10:1–5; Exodus 37:1–2)
3. the four world empires to come (Daniel 7)
4. d (Proverbs 6:6–8)
5. the foundations (Revelation 21:1–21)

Day 295

1. What man, attempting to steady the ark of the covenant on its cart, was struck dead for touching it?

2. What sin was mentioned specifically in the decree written by the king that ordered the people of Nineveh to repent?
   a) adultery
   b) idolatry
   c) usury
   d) violence

3. Which of the churches of Revelation did Jesus criticize for tolerating "that woman Jezebel"?

4. Match: Worship of Baal. . .
   a) Elijah's fire consumed even the stones and the soil.
   b) The prophets of Baal stopped shouting at midday.
   c) The prophets of Baal got a little fire going, but then it went out.

5. What king solicited the services of the witch of Endor?

ANSWERS

1. Uzzah (2 Samuel 6:6–7)
2. d (Jonah 3:6–8)
3. Thyatira (Revelation 2:18–20)
4. a (1 Kings 18:36–38)
5. Saul (1 Samuel 28:7–25)

Day 296

1. What did Jesus tell His disciples they were "the salt of"?

2. Connect the Thoughts:
    bread upon waters
    a time for everything
    "vanity of vanities"

3. Complete Jesus' sentence: "For out of the overflow of the _____ the mouth speaks."

4. According to the apostle Paul, what "governmental" role do believers play for Christ?
    a) tax collectors
    b) governors
    c) ambassadors
    d) commissioners

5. Under what two places did Jesus say that a lamp should not be put?

ANSWERS

1. the earth (Matthew 5:13 NIV)
2. the book of Ecclesiastes (Ecclesiastes 11:1; Ecclesiastes 3:1; Ecclesiastes 1:2 KJV)
3. heart (Matthew 12:34 NIV)
4. c (2 Corinthians 5:20)
5. basket, bed (Mark 4:21)

Day 297

1. What son of Jared lived "only" 365 years but didn't die—because God took him away?

2. How many days' warning of the destruction to come did God give Nineveh?

3. Connect the Thoughts:
   a fruit of the Spirit
   Jesus gives not as the world gives
   something to pray for Jerusalem

4. What kind of tree did a man named Zacchaeus climb in order to see Jesus?

5. The book of Ecclesiastes contains mostly
   a) history.
   b) law.
   c) movie reviews.
   d) words of wisdom.

ANSWERS

1. Enoch (Genesis 5:18, 23–24; Hebrews 11:5)
2. forty (Jonah 3:4)
3. peace (Galatians 5:22–23; John 14:27; Psalm 122:6)
4. sycamore-fig, or sycomore (Luke 19:1–4)
5. d

Day 298

1. In his letter to the Colossians, Paul writes that in Christ "the fullness of the ____ lives in bodily form."

2. True or False: Jesus mentioned the people of Nineveh in His teaching.

3. What kind of tomb did Jesus derisively use to describe the hypocritical Pharisees and teachers of the law?

4. Jesus taught in parables so
   a) those who didn't love God wouldn't understand His teachings.
   b) He could put them together later in a book.
   c) His disciples could sell the rights to them after His resurrection.
   d) He would be famous.

5. Complete the scripture:
[Jesus said,] As long as I am in the world, I am the ____ of the world.

ANSWERS

1. Deity (Colossians 2:9 NIV)
2. True (Matthew 12:41; Luke 11:32)
3. whitewashed, or whited (Matthew 23:27–28)
4. a (Matthew 13:11–13)
5. light (John 9:5 KJV)

Day 299

1. What did Joseph do during the years when there was plenty of food?

2. What priest of Midian was father-in-law to Moses?

3. Connect the Thoughts:
   father of Obed
   great-grandfather of King David
   husband of Ruth

4. Match: Asa. . .
   a) He erected Asherah poles and set up an altar for Baal.
   b) He deposed his grandmother for setting up an Asherah pole.
   c) During his reign there were no wars.

5. What did Samson challenge his wedding banquet guests to do?

ANSWERS

1. stored food for the future (Genesis 41:46–48)
2. Jethro (Exodus 3:1)
3. Boaz (Ruth 4:13–22)
4. b (1 Kings 15:11–13 NIV)
5. He challenged them to solve a riddle (Judges 14:10–13).

Day 300

1. What is the last event recorded in Genesis?
    a) Joseph's death
    b) Abraham's death
    c) Sarah's death
    d) Rebekah's death

2. How long was Lazarus in the tomb before Jesus arrived at the site in Bethany?

3. After Gideon's death, Israel
    a) remained faithful to the Lord for the next fourscore and three years.
    b) enjoyed peace for three generations.
    c) began building a temple to the one true God.
    d) returned to worshiping false gods.

4. Match: Jesus' trial. . .
    a) He appeared first before Annas.
    b) He appeared first before Caiaphas.
    c) He appeared first before the Sanhedrin.

5. What coming day, according to the Proverbs, shows the worthlessness of wealth?

ANSWERS

1. a (Genesis 50:26)
2. four days (John 11:17)
3. d (Judges 8:33)
4. a (John 18:12–13)
5. the day of wrath (Proverbs 11:4)

Day 301

1. Besides the Counselor, or the Holy Spirit, that Jesus promised to send to testify about Him, whom did Jesus say should testify?

2. According to David, how far has God "removed our transgressions from us"?
   a) as far as the east is from the west
   b) as far as the earth is from the stars
   c) as far as a man can travel
   d) as far as the light can pierce the darkness

3. What, according to the psalmist, declare the glory of God?

4. God restored unto Job
   a) three daughters and seven sons.
   b) seven daughters and three sons.
   c) ten beautiful daughters.
   d) ten handsome sons.

5. In Ecclesiastes 12:13, what does the Bible say is the whole duty of man?

ANSWERS

1. His believers (John 15:27)
2. a (Psalm 103:12)
3. the heavens (Psalm 19:1)
4. a (Job 42:12–13)
5. Fear God and keep His commandments.

Day 302

1. Who urged Pontius Pilate to leave Jesus alone after having a dream about Him?

2. Connect the Thoughts:
   Philippi
   purple cloth
   convert of Paul

3. Whom did Jesus describe as "a true Israelite, in whom there is nothing false"?

4. Match: Stephen. . .
   a) disciple exiled to Patmos
   b) member of the Synagogue of the Freedmen
   c) one of seven disciples chosen to distribute food

5. Who were the two women Paul urged to get along together in Philippians 4:2?

ANSWERS

1. Pilate's wife (Matthew 27:17–19)
2. Lydia (Acts 16:12–15)
3. His disciple Nathanael (John 1:47 NIV)
4. c (Acts 6:1–5)
5. Euodias and Syntyche (Philippians 4:2)

Day 303

1. What city was the site of King Xerxes's royal citadel?

2. Connect the Thoughts:
   Pison, or Pishon
   Hiddekel, or Tigris
   Euphrates

3. At what place, whose name means "oil press," did three disciples fall asleep?

4. Match: Crossing the Jordan. . .carrying the ark of the covenant entered the water first.
   a) The priests
   b) The water was less than a foot deep and placid.
   c) Moses led the people across the Jordan.

5. From what land were the traders that bought Joseph from his brothers?

ANSWERS

1. Susa, or Shushan (Esther 1:2)
2. rivers of Eden (Genesis 2:10–14)
3. Gethsemane (Matthew 26:36, 43)
4. a (Joshua 3:14–15)
5. Midian (Genesis 37:28)

Day 304

1. As the perfect Son of God, what does Jesus offer to all who obey Him?

2. Jesus offered Himself as a sacrifice for the church, to make the church ___. What *H* word is missing?

3. When did Jesus say that the disciples would be witnesses to Him?

4. How did Jesus calm a storm on the sea?
   a) He spoke to the storm.
   b) He touched the water with a stick.
   c) He waved His arms over the sea.
   d) He dipped His robe into the water.

5. Whom did Jesus say is the only one that should be called "teacher"?

ANSWERS

1. eternal salvation; everlasting life (Hebrews 5:8–9)
2. holy (Ephesians 5:25–26)
3. after the Holy Spirit came upon them (Acts 1:8)
4. a (Mark 4:39)
5. the Christ (Matthew 23:10)

Day 305

1. What green stone resembles the rainbow circling God's throne in heaven?

2. Connect the Thoughts:
   the prodigal son
   Legion
   casting pearls

3. Who dreamed of seven skinny cows eating seven fat cows?

4. What type of tree surrounded a man on a red horse in a vision of the prophet Zechariah?
   a) oak
   b) cedar
   c) maple
   d) myrtle

5. What is one of the two kinds of birds a poor person could substitute for a lamb when making sacrifice for sin?

ANSWERS

1. emerald (Revelation 4:1–3)
2. swine, or pigs (Luke 15:11–16; Mark 5:9–13; Matthew 7:6)
3. Pharaoh (Genesis 41)
4. d (Zechariah 1:7–8)
5. dove or pigeon (Leviticus 5:6–7)

Day 306

1. False prophets
    a) lie.
    b) disrespect God.
    c) tell people what they want to hear.
    d) all of the above.

2. What prophet confronted David about his sins toward Uriah?

3. True or False: The men who brought to Jesus a woman caught in adultery really wanted to know His thoughts on the law.

4. Connect the Thoughts:
    the seventh commandment
    a lustful look
    divorcing to remarry

5. Micah said the people wanted a prophet who would
    a) lie.
    b) cheat.
    c) steal.
    d) sing.

ANSWERS

1. d (2 Peter 2:1–3)
2. Nathan (2 Samuel 12:1–10)
3. False. They were trying to trick Jesus (John 8:6).
4. adultery (Exodus 20:3–17; Matthew 5:28; Matthew 19:9)
5. a (Micah 2:11)

Day 307

1. What does Proverbs say is the "beginning of wisdom"?

2. Complete Jesus' sentence: "Now that I, your Lord and ____ , have washed your feet, you also should wash one another's feet."

3. To what liquid did both Paul and Peter liken the Word?
   a) milk
   b) oil
   c) water
   d) wine

4. Complete the scripture:
   And he saith unto them, Follow me, and I will make you ____ of men.

5. What three hazards befell the seeds in Jesus' parable of the sower?

ANSWERS

1. the fear of the Lord (Proverbs 9:10 NIV)
2. Teacher (John 13:14 NIV)
3. a (1 Corinthians 3:1–2; 1 Peter 1:25–2:2)
4. fishers (Matthew 4:19 KJV)
5. birds, the sun, thorns (Matthew 13:4–7)

Day 308

1. The Israelites built for the Egyptians
   a) the Tower of Babel.
   b) a synagogue.
   c) the Eiffel Tower.
   d) treasure cities.

2. What, according to Revelation, is the "number of the beast"?

3. Connect the Thoughts:
   Reuben, to Jacob
   Esau, to Isaac
   lost in the last plague on Egypt

4. What famous tree of Lebanon was used by the psalmist as a metaphor for the righteous?

5. Match: Stairway of Ahaz. . .
   a) a stone formation
   b) a sundial
   c) a constellation

ANSWERS

1. d (Exodus 1:9–11 KJV)
2. 666 (Revelation 13:18)
3. firstborn sons (Genesis 46:8; Genesis 27:19–20; Exodus 12:29–30)
4. cedar (Psalm 92:12)
5. b (2 Kings 20:11)

Day 309

1. Jesus told Martha that
   a) Mary was indeed very, very lazy.
   b) Mary wasn't very interesting anyway.
   c) He would buy her a new vase.
   d) she should allow Mary to listen to His Word.

2. How many people did Jesus appoint to go, two by two, ahead of Him to various towns to prepare the way for Jesus Himself?

3. True or False: Peter says that when we live like Jesus, we will not live like the rest of the world lives.

4. Where in the Old Testament is the prophecy about Jesus being "bruised," or "crushed," "for our iniquities"?

5. Jesus teaches we should
   a) not do anything extra for our enemies but the bare minmum.
   b) love our friends more than our enemies.
   c) give our enemies New Testament Bibles.
   d) go the extra mile for our enemies and to show them much love.

ANSWERS

1. d (Luke 10:41–42)
2. Seventy-two (Luke 10:1 NIV)
3. True (1 Peter 1:13–16)
4. Isaiah 53
5. d (Luke 6:29)

Day 310

1. What trio of friends offered Job plenty of advice but little comfort throughout his trials?

2. Connect the Thoughts:
   Mahlon
   Elimelech
   Naomi

3. What two Israelite spies were commended for the way they "wholly followed the Lord"—as opposed to ten other spies who gave a bad report on the land of Canaan?

4. Match: Joash. . .
   a) He was hidden for six years from his grandmother.
   b) He removed all the high places and idols during his reign.
   c) He was eight years old when he began his reign.

5. Who found the baby Moses?

ANSWERS

1. Eliphaz, Bildad, and Zophar (Job 2:11 and following)
2. characters in the story of Ruth (Ruth 1:1–5)
3. Caleb and Joshua (Numbers 13:26–33, 32:12 KJV)
4. a (2 Kings 11:1–3)
5. Pharaoh's daughter (Exodus 2:5–6, 10)

Day 311

1. At what occasion was Jesus speaking when He said, "I will not drink of this fruit of the vine. . .until that day when I drink it anew with you in my Father's kingdom"?

2. Peter healed Aeneas from
    a) palsy.
    b) leprosy.
    c) lameness.
    d) demon possession.

3. Complete the scripture:
The Lord himself shall descend from heaven with a shout, with the voice of the archangel, and with the trump of God: and the ___ ___ ___ shall rise first.

4. To whom must the gospel of Jesus Christ be preached before the end of the world comes, according to Matthew's Gospel?

5. Jesus' first miracle was important because it strengthened the faith of
    a) Jesus' disciples.
    b) Jesus' earthly mother and father.
    c) His earthly sisters and brothers.
    d) the townspeople of Cana.

ANSWERS

1. the Last Supper (Matthew 26:17–29 NIV)
2. a (Acts 9:32–34)
3. dead in Christ (1 Thessalonians 4:16 KJV)
4. the whole world (Matthew 24:14)
5. a (John 2:11)

Day 312

1. Connect the Thoughts:
   Holy One of Israel
   the Father of lights
   I Am

2. What did God tell Moses would keep the diseases of the Egyptians from afflicting the Israelites?

3. True or False: God wants animal sacrifices from Christians.

4. What two words, according to John, describe God in forgiving and cleansing, "if we confess our sins"?

5. Complete the scripture:
   Whether therefore ye eat, or drink, or whatsoever ye do, do all to the ___ of God.

ANSWERS

1. names of God (Psalm 71:22; James 1:17; Exodus 3:14)
2. diligently keeping God's commands (Exodus 15:26)
3. False. God wants us to have a relationship with Him (Micah 6:8).
4. faithful, just (1 John 1:9)
5. glory (1 Corinthians 10:31 KJV)

Day 313

1. What was the relationship of Onesimus to the New Testament letter recipient Philemon?

2. Connect the Thoughts:
   Joseph, or Joses, from Cyprus
   an argument with Paul
   regarded as a god

3. What occupation did the apostle Paul have in addition to his missionary duties?

4. Match: Silas. . .
   a) went to Athens initially with Paul.
   b) helped write the book of James.
   c) was in jail with Paul in Philippi.

5. Whom did the people of Lystra insist that Paul and Barnabas were?

ANSWERS

1. slave (Philemon 1, 10–16)
2. Barnabas (Acts 4:36; Acts 15:39–40; Acts 14:8–12)
3. tentmaker (Acts 18:1–3)
4. c (Acts 16:22–40)
5. Jupiter and Mercurius (Acts 14:12 KJV) or Zeus and Hermes (NIV)

Day 314

1. What mount is associated with the heavenly Jerusalem?

2. Philippi was
   a) a country in Asia.
   b) a city in Macedonia.
   c) an island in the Mediterranean.
   d) a village near Bethlehem.

3. The ancestors of what two warring nations fought together before they were born?

4. Match: Nile. . .
   a) where baby Moses was hidden
   b) turned to mud by Moses
   c) also known as the Great Sea

5. Where was Ezekiel when he began to prophesy?

ANSWERS

1. Zion, or Sion (Hebrews 12:22)
2. b (Acts 16:12)
3. Israelites (Jacob) and Edomites (Esau) (Genesis 25:21–26)
4. a (Exodus 2:1–3, 5–10)
5. Babylon (Ezekiel 1:3 NIV)

Day 315

1. Before Jesus ascended into heaven, He told His disciples they would be His witnesses in Jerusalem, in all Judea and Samaria, and where else?

2. True or False: When a village in Samaria refused to receive Jesus, the disciples pleaded with Jesus to forgive the people of the village.

3. To what time in the Old Testament did Jesus compare the time when the Son of Man will return?

4. Complete the scripture:
The water that I shall give him shall be in him a well of water springing up into ___ life.

5. What will our Savior, the Lord Jesus Christ, do to our bodies once we join Him in heaven?

ANSWERS

1. "to the ends of the earth" (Acts 1:8 NIV)
2. False (Luke 9:51–54)
3. the days of Noah (Matthew 24:37)
4. everlasting (John 4:14 KJV)
5. They will be transformed to appear like Jesus' glorious body (Philippians 3:21).

Day 316

1. What sparkling substance does the writer of Proverbs compare to the poison of a viper?

2. What happened to Aaron's golden calf?

3. We will know that the kingdom of God is near, Jesus says, speaking in a parable, when what kind of tree sprouts leaves?
   a) apple
   b) fig
   c) oak
   d) olive

4. What term, meaning "one who bears blame," described a sacrificial goat chosen by lot to be set free in the desert?

5. What coin did the householder agree to pay each laborer for a day's work in his vineyard?

ANSWERS

1. wine (Proverbs 23:31–32)
2. It was ground into powder and mixed with water, and the people were forced to drink it (Exodus 32:2–4, 20).
3. b (Luke 21:29–31)
4. scapegoat (Leviticus 16:6–10)
5. penny, or denarius (Matthew 20:2)

Day 317

1. What word describes how Peter wept after denying the Lord three times?

2. Jesus said the merchants in the temple had made it a
    a) Cub Scout den.
    b) den of snakes.
    c) den of bears.
    d) den of thieves.

3. After his sin, David married Bathsheba and a son was born. What was his name?

4. Match: Lucifer. . .
    a) Lucius
    b) Lucas
    c) Satan

5. Why didn't the soldiers on watch at the tomb admit that the Son of God had risen?

ANSWERS

1. bitterly (Matthew 26:75)
2. d (Mark 11:17)
3. Solomon (2 Samuel 12:24)
4. c (Isaiah 14:12–15 KJV)
5. They were bribed by the chief priests and elders to say that Jesus' disciples stole His body (Matthew 28:11–15).

Day 318

1. What five-word phrase did the apostle Paul say he had become in his efforts to bring various people to Christ?

2. According to the Proverbs, what are we not to "lean on"?
    a) a crooked staff
    b) our own understanding
    c) a double-minded man
    d) the riches of this world

3. Just as we cannot live in light and darkness at the same time, Jesus says we cannot serve two masters. Complete Jesus' sentence: "You cannot serve both God and ___."

4. What did the apostle Paul call the nine-fold characteristics (love, joy, peace, etc.) of the maturing Christian?
    a) the harvest of faith
    b) the works of the righteous
    c) the fruit of the Spirit
    d) the life of Christ

5. In Micah 6:8, what does the Lord require of us?

ANSWERS

1. all things to all men (1 Corinthians 9:22 NIV)
2. b (Proverbs 3:5)
3. money (Matthew 6:24 NIV)
4. c (Galatians 5:22–23)
5. to do justly, to love mercy, and to walk humbly with your God

Day 319

1. Who wrote down the book of Romans for the apostle Paul?
   a) Lucius
   b) Jason
   c) Tertius
   d) Erastus

2. What symbolic act did Pontius Pilate perform to try to brush aside responsibility for Jesus' crucifixion?

3. Connect the Thoughts:
   a kiss
   scriptures
   Spirit

4. In the new Jerusalem, only those whose names are written where will be allowed to enter?

5. Match: Publius. . .
   a) Greek silversmith
   b) chief official on Malta
   c) Greek preacher in the early church

ANSWERS

1. c (Romans 16:22)
2. he washed his hands (Matthew 27:24)
3. things described as "holy" (2 Corinthians 13:12; 2 Timothy 3:15; Acts 2:4)
4. in the Lamb's book of life (Revelation 21:1, 27)
5. b (Acts 28:1, 7)

Day 320

1. What agricultural term did Jesus use to describe the soul-winners' goal?

2. Quoting the Old Testament—"I desire mercy, not sacrifice"—Jesus proclaimed to the Pharisees that He was Lord of the ____.

3. According to Matthew, what phenomenon accompanied both the death and resurrection of Jesus?
   a) lightning
   b) howling wind
   c) an earthquake
   d) an eclipse

4. True or False: Jesus' disciples wondered who would be the most important among themselves in heaven.

5. What did Mark quote Jesus as saying everyone would be "salted with"?

ANSWERS

1. harvest (Luke 10:1–2)
2. Sabbath (Matthew 12:2, 7–8 NIV)
3. c (Matthew 27:51, 28:2)
4. True (Luke 9:46)
5. fire (Mark 9:49 NIV)

Day 321

1. Before the Israelites left Egypt, God told them to ask for
   a) manna.
   b) milk and honey.
   c) thirty shekels each.
   d) silver and gold.

2. What son of Saul loved his friend David "as himself"?

3. Connect the Thoughts:
   a tiller of the ground
   a murderer
   a marked man

4. Match: Lot. . .
   a) The angels wanted to spend the night at Lot's house.
   b) Lot's sons-in-law invited the angels to their houses.
   c) The angels blinded the men of Sodom.

5. Where was Pharaoh's daughter when she found baby Moses?

ANSWERS

1. d (Exodus 11:1–2)
2. Jonathan (1 Samuel 18:1)
3. Cain (Genesis 4:2–15)
4. c (Genesis 19:1–2, 11)
5. at the river, getting ready to take a bath (Exodus 2:5–6, 10)

Day 322

1. After Pentecost, when Peter and other apostles were arrested and put in jail, who set them free during the night?

2. When a person who was not a disciple cast out demons in Jesus' name, the disciples
    a) told him to stop.
    b) rejoiced.
    c) told him to be wary of demons.
    d) tried to take credit.

3. At what hour do three Gospel writers say the Son of Man will come again?

4. Stephen answered the charge against him
    a) by suing his accusers for ruining his reputation.
    b) by vowing to murder his enemies.
    c) by throwing himself on the mercy of the court.
    d) by giving a speech in defense of Christianity.

5. True or False: Stephen praised Israel during his court appearance.

ANSWERS

1. an angel of the Lord (Acts 5:17–19)
2. a (Luke 9:49)
3. at an hour when you do not expect Him (Matthew 24:44; Mark 13:33; Luke 21:34)
4. d (Acts 7:1–53)
5. False (Acts 7:51–53)

Day 323

1. What psalm mentions the law of the Lord in every verse?

2. To prove to Moses the people would know he had seen Him, God used a
   a) shepherd's rod.
   b) talking frog.
   c) vision.
   d) golden calf.

3. Who was known as the friend of God?

4. True or False: Obeying God's commandment not to take His name in vain is one way to keep God's name hallowed.

5. What did the people think would happen to them if God, instead of Moses, spoke to them?

ANSWERS

1. Psalm 119
2. a (Exodus 4:1–5)
3. Abraham (James 2:23)
4. True
5. They would die (Exodus 20:18–19).

Day 324

1. Who gave up his own new tomb for the burial of the crucified Jesus?

2. Connect the Thoughts:
   Tiberius
   Claudius
   Augustus

3. What was the name of the Pharisee who ordered that the apostles not be put to death but rather freed to go their way?

4. Match: Julius. . .
   a) apostle who was in prison with Paul
   b) inventor of the harp and flute
   c) Roman centurion who saved Paul's life

5. Who rejected Jesus' offer of eternal life because he wouldn't give up what he had?

ANSWERS

1. Joseph of Arimathea (Matthew 27:57–60)
2. caesars (Luke 3:1; Acts 11:28; Luke 2:1)
3. Gamaliel (Acts 5:34–39)
4. c (Acts 27:1, 43)
5. the rich young ruler (Matthew 19:21–24)

Day 325

1. What mountain did Moses climb to see the Promised Land he would not be allowed to enter?

2. Connect the Thoughts:
   a closet
   Gethsemane
   inside a fish

3. Where was the Pool of Bethesda?

4. Match: Galilee. . .
   a) where Jesus was baptized
   b) where Jesus first met Matthew
   c) where Jesus walked on water

5. Where was Paul, experiencing a nighttime vision of a man, invited to spread the gospel?

ANSWERS

1. Pisgah (Deuteronomy 3:21–29)
2. places of prayer (Matthew 6:6 KJV; Mark 14:32; Jonah 2:1)
3. by the Sheep Gate in Jerusalem (John 5:2–4 KJV)
4. c (John 6:1, 16–21)
5. Macedonia (Acts 16:9–10)

Day 326

1. True or False: Peter is considered to be the leader of Jesus' twelve disciples.

2. What did the bread and wine at Jesus' last supper with His disciples symbolize?

3. True or False: Jesus predicted His own death and resurrection.

4. How did Jesus, by His example in the wilderness, show us to resist Satan?

5. Jesus' enemies did not want him arrested during the Feast of Unleavened Bread because they
   a) wanted Jesus to miss out on all the good food.
   b) wanted Jesus to turn water into wine for them.
   c) were afraid the Jews might riot.
   d) were afraid that would ruin their celebration.

ANSWERS

1. True (Matthew 16:18)
2. His body and blood, which were to be sacrificed for them (and us) (Luke 22:19–20).
3. True (Luke 9:21-22)
4. He quoted scriptures to him (Matthew 4:1-11).
5. c (Matthew 26:2–5)

Day 327

1. What kind of bird did God miraculously provide for the Israelites, who had grown tired of manna?

2. What builder's tool did God show Amos to indicate Israel's coming judgment?
   a) a chisel
   b) a hammer
   c) a trowel
   d) a plumb line

3. What two grains did Ruth glean?

4. What color of heifer—which had never worn a yoke—were Moses and Aaron instructed to sacrifice?
   a) red
   b) gray
   c) brown
   d) black

5. What two animals appeared in a prophetic vision of Daniel's, near the Ulai Canal?

ANSWERS

1. quail (Numbers 11:31–32)
2. d (Amos 7:1–9)
3. barley and wheat (Ruth 2:23)
4. a (Numbers 19:1–5)
5. ram and goat (Daniel 8:1–12)

Day 328

1. What man's desertion from the gospel ministry caused a falling out between the apostle Paul and his coworker Barnabas?

2. During the plagues, God turned the water of the Nile into
   a) blood.
   b) wine.
   c) milk.
   d) honey.

3. What book of the Bible lists the seven deadly sins?

4. Hatred stirs anger, but sin is covered by
   a) hate.
   b) anger.
   c) love.
   d) slime.

5. What did Haman plan to do to all the Jews?

ANSWERS

1. John Mark (Acts 15:36–40)
2. a (Exodus 7:20)
3. none—they're not in the Bible
4. c (Proverbs 10:12)
5. destroy them (Esther 3:8–9)

Day 329

1. What did the apostle Paul, writing to the Thessalonians, say that those who refused to work should be kept from doing?

2. Complete Paul's sentence: "So, whether we live or die, we belong to the _____."

3. Match: The kingdom of heaven. . .
   a) is like a field of flowers.
   b) is like a merchant who finds a pearl.
   c) is like a fishing boat.

4. In Jesus' illustration of how God wants to give us good things, what did the Lord say a father would *not* give his son if he asked for bread?

5. What does Psalm 118:24 say we are to do with this day the Lord has made?

ANSWERS

1. eating (2 Thessalonians 3:10)
2. Lord (Romans 14:8 NIV)
3. b (Matthew 13:45)
4. a stone (Luke 11:11–13)
5. rejoice and be glad in it

Day 330

1. What phrase from the book of Genesis describes the marriage of a man and a woman?
   a) one flesh
   b) holy union
   c) children of God
   d) great reward

2. What color hair, according to the Proverbs, is the "splendor of the old"?

3. True or False: The original stone tablets on which the Ten Commandments were written are thought to exist to this day, but archaeologists have been unable to find them.

4. What is the name of the star that falls to earth and poisons a third of the water, as described in Revelation?

5. Match: Festus. . .
   a) presented religious leaders' charges against Paul to governor of Judea.
   b) succeeded Felix as governor of Judea.
   c) was married to Drusilla, a Jewish woman.

ANSWERS

1. a (Genesis 2:24)
2. gray (Proverbs 20:29 NIV)
3. False. Moses broke them in anger when the Israelites disobeyed God by making and worshiping a golden calf (Exodus 32:19).
4. Wormwood (Revelation 8:10–11)
5. b (Acts 24:27)

Day 331

1. True or False: In Matthew's Gospel, Jesus told the disciples how to pray because He was angered by the hypocrites' loud praying.

2. What type of tree immediately withered when Jesus cursed it—an event Jesus used to teach His disciples about faith?

3. Connect the Thoughts:
   "I thirst."
   "Father, forgive them."
   "Why hast thou forsaken me?"

4. What proof does Paul offer that Jesus is holy?

5. True or False: Jesus revered his mother, Mary, over everyone else.

ANSWERS

1. True (Matthew 6:5)
2. fig (Matthew 21:18–22)
3. sayings of Jesus on the cross (John 19:28 KJV; Luke 23:34 KJV; Mark 15:34 KJV)
4. Jesus' resurrection from the dead (Romans 1:4)
5. False (Luke 8:19–21)

Day 332

1. What king of Persia permitted the Jews in his realm to return to Jerusalem to rebuild the temple?

2. Connect the Thoughts:
   700 wives
   1,005 songs
   3,000 proverbs

3. What did Samson do to make good on his promise to give thirty people fine cloaks?

4. Match: Balaam. . .
   a) He beat his donkey three times, whenever the angel appeared.
   b) The angel told him to say anything to Balak.
   c) The angel broke his arm.

5. What name, meaning "bitter," did Ruth's newly-widowed mother-in-law give herself?

ANSWERS

1. Cyrus (Ezra 1:1–4)
2. Solomon (1 Kings 11:1–3; 1 Kings 4:32)
3. He went to the next Philistine town, slew thirty men, and took their cloaks (Judges 14:12, 18–19).
4. a (Numbers 22:27–28, 32)
5. Mara (Ruth 1:20)

Day 333

1. Before what event in His earthly life did Jesus wash His disciples' feet?

2. The Day of Atonement gave Israelites the opportunity to
   a) eat a great feast.
   b) sleep in.
   c) tone their muscles.
   d) make amends for their sins.

3. What does Zechariah say will happen when the Messiah's foot touches the Mount of Olives?

4. A dispute arose in the early church which concerned
   a) gleaning the fields for leftover harvest.
   b) Stephen's marriage.
   c) who would own the rights to broadcast films of Jesus' sermons.
   d) the widows' portion of bread.

5. What three-word question did Pontius Pilate utter after Jesus said He had come into the world to testify to the truth?

ANSWERS

1. on the night before His crucifixion (John 13:1, 5)
2. d (Leviticus 23:27–28)
3. The mountain will split in two (Zechariah 14:4)
4. d (Acts 6:1)
5. "What is truth?" (John 18:37–38 NIV)

Day 334

1. To whom does Jude give praise and glory?

2. According to the psalmist, God owns what on a thousand hills?
   a) the cell phone towers
   b) the cattle
   c) the dwellings
   d) the oak trees

3. Who was known as the man after God's own heart?

4. After Job's suffering, God
   a) gave Job twice as much as he had before his suffering.
   b) gave Job three times as much as he had before his suffering.
   c) gave Job four times as much as he had before his suffering.
   d) gave Job nothing.

5. What, according to Psalm 19, are God's laws to be desired more than?

ANSWERS

1. God (Jude 25)
2. b (Psalm 50:10)
3. David (1 Samuel 13:14; Acts 13:22)
4. a (Job 42:10)
5. much fine gold (Psalm 19:7–10)

Day 335

1. Who addressed the Sanhedrin with a face like an angel?

2. What second name was Thomas known by?

3. Match: Judas. . .
   a) Jesus gave him a piece of bread dipped in a dish.
   b) He was called a "lion's cub" by Jacob.
   c) He was a candidate, with Matthias, to become a disciple.

4. Who was commanded to go lay hands on Saul (Paul) so that he would regain his sight?

5. To what political party did Jesus' disciple Simon belong?

ANSWERS

1. Stephen (Acts 6:8, 15)
2. Didymus (John 11:16)
3. a (John 13:26)
4. Ananias (Acts 9:10–18)
5. He was a Zealot (Luke 6:15; Acts 1:13).

Day 336

1. What "mighty hunter" built Nineveh shortly after Noah's time?

2. Connect the Thoughts:
   wine mingled with myrrh
   the Crucifixion
   "the place of a skull"

3. Match:. River of Life. . .
   a) in the new Jerusalem
   b) another name for the Tigris
   c) another name for the Jordan

4. When Naomi and Ruth arrived in Bethlehem, Naomi
   a) changed her name to Mara.
   b) got a new Social Security number.
   c) burned incense to Jehovah.
   d) told everyone that they were following a star.

5. Where did Jesus begin His ministry?

ANSWERS

1. Nimrod (Genesis 10:8–11)
2. Golgotha (Mark 15:22–23; John 19:16–18)
3. a (Revelation 21:2, 22:1)
4. a (Ruth 1:19–20)
5. Galilee (Luke 4:14)

Day 337

1. What notice did Pilate have prepared and fastened to Jesus' cross?

2. Some important people were mad at Jesus because He ate with
   a) tax collectors and outcasts.
   b) no one—He ate alone.
   c) His family instead of them.
   d) His favorite disciples.

3. True or False: Jesus had no followers who were women.

4. What did Jesus say the Pharisees would see in response to their demand for a sign from heaven?

5. Complete the scripture:
   Therefore being justified by faith, we have ___ with God through our Lord Jesus Christ.

ANSWERS

1. Jesus of Nazareth, the King of the Jews (John 19:19 NIV)
2. a (Luke 5:30)
3. False (Luke 8:1–3)
4. the sign of Jonah, or Jonas (Matthew 16:1–4)
5. peace (Romans 5:1 KJV)

Day 338

1. How many precious stones, representing the tribes of Israel, were part of the breastplate worn by Old Testament priests?

2. Which minor prophet prophesied that the Messiah would be born in Bethlehem?
   a) Joel
   b) Micah
   c) Amos
   d) Zechariah

3. What did Joseph dream the sun, the moon, and eleven stars did?

4. Match: Venison. . .
   a) Daniel's diet for seven days
   b) one of Isaac's favorite dishes
   c) what manna tasted like

5. What kind of tree was Gideon working under when the angel of the Lord greeted him?

ANSWERS

1. twelve (Exodus 28:15–21)
2. b (Micah 5:2)
3. They bowed down to him (Genesis 37:9–11).
4. b (Genesis 25:28)
5. oak (Judges 6:11–12)

Day 339

1. What is the name that means "wickedness," which is referred to in the Old Testament as being a father to children who worship other gods?

2. For what offense did Elisha curse some young people of Bethel, resulting in the mauling of forty-two youth by bears?
    a) desecrating the temple
    b) using the Lord's name in vain
    c) immorality
    d) making fun of his baldness

3. Why, according to Jesus, have men loved darkness instead of light?

4. After Samson lied to her, Delilah
    a) gave up.
    b) pestered Samson every day to tell her until he confessed.
    c) lied to the Philistine lords and collected her money.
    d) threw a fit.

5. Whose spirit was brought up from the dead by the witch of Endor?

ANSWERS

1. Belial (Deuteronomy 13:13)
2. d (2 Kings 2:23–24)
3. Because their deeds were evil (John 3:19).
4. b (Judges 16:16–17)
5. Samuel (1 Samuel 28:7–25)

Day 340

1. What adjective, besides "peaceful," or "peaceable," describes the kind of Christian life Paul told Timothy to live?

2. How, according to the apostle Paul, are Christians to pray?
   a) without pride
   b) without ceasing
   c) without hypocrisy
   d) without wavering

3. Complete Jesus' sentence from a parable: "The kingdom of heaven is like ____ that a woman took and mixed into a large amount of flour until it worked all through the dough."

4. In Ephesians 6, what do we not wrestle against?

5. What did Paul tell Timothy to fight?

ANSWERS

1. quiet (1 Timothy 2:1–2)
2. b (1 Thessalonians 5:17)
3. yeast (Matthew 13:33 NIV)
4. flesh and blood (Ephesians 6:12)
5. the good fight of faith (1 Timothy 6:12)

Day 341

1. How many silver coins did Judas Iscariot receive for betraying Jesus?

2. Connect the Thoughts:
   Joseph in Egypt
   Cyrenius, or Quirinius, in Syria
   Pontius Pilate in Judea

3. What is the last verse of the Bible?

4. Match: Hophni and Phineas. . .
   a) Eli's sons, who died on the same day
   b) Moses' sons, who were circumcised by their mother
   c) Samuel's sons, who disobeyed God

5. What two books of the Bible mention the tree of life?

ANSWERS

1. thirty (Matthew 27:3–4)
2. governors (Genesis 42:1–6; Luke 2:2; Luke 3:1)
3. "The grace of our Lord Jesus Christ be with you all. Amen" (Revelation 22:21 KJV).
4. a (1 Samuel 2:34, 4:11)
5. Genesis and Revelation (Genesis 2:9, 3:22, 3:24; Revelation 2:7, 22:14)

Day 342

1. To whom is Jesus speaking when He says, "For this reason I was born, and for this I came into the world, to testify to the truth. Everyone on the side of truth listens to me"?

2. Connect the Thoughts:
   the Bread of Life
   the True Vine
   Alpha and Omega

3. When Jesus read in the synagogue, from what book of the Old Testament did He read?

4. Who initially scoffed at Jesus, saying, "Nazareth! Can anything good come from there?"
   a) Peter
   b) Philip
   c) John
   d) Nathanael

5. True or False: Jesus turned stones into bread to show the devil He was God's Son.

ANSWERS

1. Pontius Pilate (John 18:37 NIV)
2. "I am" statements of Jesus (John 6:35; John 15:1; Revelation 1:8)
3. Isaiah (Luke 4:14–18)
4. d (John 1:46 NIV)
5. False (Matthew 4:4)

Day 343

1. Which tribe of Israel, set apart to be priests, did not receive part of the Promised Land, since "the Lord is their inheritance"?

2. What construction project did Nehemiah bring to a successful conclusion despite the mocking and threats of enemies?
   a) the tower of David
   b) the temple
   c) King Solomon's palace
   d) the wall of Jerusalem

3. What did each of Nehemiah's workers keep by his side during the construction?
   a) a lamp
   b) water
   c) a sword
   d) scripture

4. Connect the Thoughts:
   the dust of the ground
   work in a garden
   names for the animals

5. Match: Nadab and Abihu. . .
   a) sons of Aaron who put fire in their censers
   b) sons of Moses who offered burnt offerings
   c) sons of Miriam who could swallow fire

ANSWERS

1. the Levites (Joshua 18:3–7)
2. d (Nehemiah 1:1–3, 6:15)
3. c (Nehemiah 4:18)
4. Adam (Genesis 2:7; Genesis 2:15; Genesis 2:19)
5. a (Leviticus 10:1–2)

Day 344

1. What phrase describes the time frame in which Christians will be changed at the sound of the last trumpet?

2. Why was Jesus' birth to Mary miraculous?
   a) She was very old.
   b) She was barren.
   c) She was a virgin.
   d) She already had twenty-two other children.

3. What event that Agabus prophesied happened in the days of Claudius Caesar?

4. During Passover, it was the custom for the ruler to
   a) renew his commitment to God.
   b) sing at the Coliseum.
   c) throw a Christian to the lions.
   d) release one prisoner.

5. True or False: Today, many Jewish people recognize the Day of Atonement.

ANSWERS

1. in a flash, in the twinkling of an eye (1 Corinthians 15:52 NIV)
2. c (Matthew 1:23)
3. a great famine throughout the world (Acts 11:28)
4. d (John 18:39)
5. True

Day 345

1. According to Paul, how should we endeavor to keep the unity of the Spirit?

2. According to the Psalms, what is "the beginning of wisdom"?
   a) the prayer of faith
   b) obedience
   c) the fear of the Lord
   d) repentance

3. How did Jesus say we are to worship God?

4. True or False: God is never mentioned by name in the book of Esther.

5. What does God promise in Isaiah 58:13–14 (NIV) to those who keep His Sabbath?

ANSWERS

1. with the bond of peace (Ephesians 4:3)
2. c (Psalm 111:10)
3. in Spirit and in truth (John 4:24)
4. True
5. They would find joy in the Lord.

Day 346

1. What Jewish ruler was told by Jesus, "You must be born again"?

2. What "eloquent man. . .mighty in the scriptures," was willing to accept the teaching of Aquila and Priscilla, who "expounded unto him the way of God more perfectly"?
   a) Luke
   b) Barnabas
   c) Titus
   d) Apollos

3. Connect the Thoughts:
   Cleopas, on the road to Emmaus
   "Doubting" Thomas
   more than five hundred believers

4. Match: Alexander. . .
   a) metalworker who harmed Timothy
   b) disciple who was sent to minister to Paul at Damascus
   c) teacher in the early church in Antioch

5. What two-word nickname—from a dreaded disease he had—described a man named Simon from Bethany?

ANSWERS

1. Nicodemus (John 3:1–7)
2. d (Acts 18:24–26 KJV)
3. people who saw Jesus after His resurrection (Luke 24:13–18; John 20:26–29; 1 Corinthians 15:3–6)
4. a (2 Timothy 4:14)
5. the Leper (Mark 14:3)

Day 347

1. What island's people welcomed the apostle Paul and 275 other people after their ship broke apart in the Adriatic Sea?

2. Connect the Thoughts:
   fewer than ten righteous people
   raining brimstone, or sulfur
   Gomorrah

3. What name—also the name of a bay in Delaware—did Isaac give to a well he dug?

4. Match: Kerith. . .
   a) where Elisha threw Elijah's cloak
   b) where Elisha met Elijah
   c) where Elijah drank from the brook

5. What enemies were Jesse's oldest boys, as members of the Israelite army, opposing in the Valley of Elah?

ANSWERS

1. Malta, or Melita (Acts 27:27–28:2)
2. Sodom (Genesis 18:22–33; Genesis 19:24)
3. Rehoboth (Genesis 26:22)
4. c (1 Kings 17:2–4 NIV)
5. Philistines (1 Samuel 17:17–19)

Day 348

1. True or False: When the baby Jesus was presented at the temple, two people said that Jesus was the Messiah.

2. What *I* word describes what Jesus is doing for us at the right hand of God, according to Paul's letter to the Romans?

3. What did Jesus say "my kingdom is not of"?
   a) the flesh
   b) silver and gold
   c) strife
   d) this world

4. What was Jesus doing in a boat immediately before calming a storm that terrified His disciples?

5. True or False: Mary selected Jesus' name herself.

ANSWERS

1. True (Luke 2:22–38)
2. interceding (Romans 8:34)
3. d (John 18:36 KJV)
4. sleeping (Luke 8:22–25)
5. False (Luke 2:21)

Day 349

1. What kind of animal did God give Abraham to sacrifice, instead of his son, Isaac?
   a) a bull
   b) a sparrow
   c) a lamb
   d) a ram

2. What round objects did Ezekiel see accompanying four strange "living creatures" in one of his visions?

3. Which one of the following animals were Israelites permitted to eat?
   a) pig
   b) camel
   c) cow
   d) rabbit

4. How many windows and doors did Noah's ark have?

5. What kind of birds fed the prophet Elijah when he was hiding from King Ahab?
   a) eagles
   b) storks
   c) hummingbirds
   d) ravens

ANSWERS

1. d (Genesis 22:13–14)
2. wheels (Ezekiel 1:15–21)
3. c (Leviticus 11:3–8)
4. one of each (Genesis 6:16)
5. d (1 Kings 17:1– 6)

Day 350

1. John writes that if we claim to have fellowship with Jesus but then choose to "walk in the darkness," we are doing what?

2. What sin had Moses committed when he was a young man in Egypt?
   a) He had called Pharaoh a bad name.
   b) He had killed an Egyptian.
   c) He had stolen Pharaoh's money.
   d) He had lied to his mother.

3. What lie did Jewish priests and Roman soldiers tell to explain the disappearance of Jesus' body after the Resurrection?

4. What part of Abel did God tell Cain "cries out to me from the ground"?

5. What kind of yoking did the apostle Paul warn the church at Corinth about?

ANSWERS

1. lying and not living by the truth (1 John 1:6)
2. b (Exodus 2:11–12)
3. that it was stolen by the disciples (Matthew 28:11–15)
4. his blood (Genesis 4:10 NIV)
5. with unbelievers, or unequal (2 Corinthians 6:14)

Day 351

1. What did Jesus say God would do for the believers He sees secretly giving to the needy?

2. Complete the scripture:
   Love ye your enemies, and do good, and lend, hoping for nothing again; and your reward shall be ____.

3. What kind of bread did Jesus teach his disciples to pray for, asking God to "give us this day"?

4. Christians should keep themselves
   a) in church at all times.
   b) on every church committee to show God how hard they work.
   c) in with the bad crowd at school.
   d) in God's love.

5. What goes before a fall, per the Proverbs?

ANSWERS

1. reward them (Matthew 6:3–4)
2. great (Luke 6:35 KJV)
3. daily (Matthew 6:11 KJV)
4. d (Jude 21)
5. a haughty spirit (Proverbs 16:18 KJV)

Day 352

1. What two things were Paul and Silas doing at midnight while imprisoned in a Philippian jail?

2. Connect the Thoughts:
   Jacob and Rachel, upon meeting
   Jonathan and David, upon parting
   Judas and Jesus, at the betrayal

3. What psalm recounts the confession of David after his sin with Bathsheba?

4. Match: Artaxerxes. . .
   a) king of Babylon who captured Zedekiah
   b) king of Persia who decreed Israelites could return to Jerusalem
   c) king of Judah who renewed covenant with God

5. What five books of the Bible have only one chapter?

ANSWERS

1. praying and singing to God (Acts 16:22–25)
2. kisses (Genesis 29:10–11; 1 Samuel 20:41–42; Mark 14:44–45)
3. Psalm 51
4. c (Ezra 7:1, 13)
5. Obadiah, Philemon, 2 John, 3 John, Jude

Day 353

1. Who assisted Joseph of Arimathea in preparing Jesus' body for burial?
   a) Zacchaeus
   b) Bartimaeus
   c) Cornelius
   d) Nicodemus

2. Complete Peter's sentence while he was speaking to the crowd at Pentecost: "God has made this Jesus, whom you crucified, both Lord and ___."

3. True or False: When Jesus appeared before Pontius Pilate, the ruler found Jesus guilty of several crimes.

4. When someone called Jesus "Good Master," what did Jesus reply?

5. Where did Jesus say His followers would never walk?
   a) in sin
   b) in sorrow
   c) in darkness
   d) in fear

ANSWERS

1. d (John 19:38–42)
2. Christ (Acts 2:36 NIV)
3. False (John 18:37–38)
4. "There is none good but. . .God" (Mark 10:17–18 KJV).
5. c (John 8:12)

Day 354

1. In exchange for betraying Samson, the Philistine lords offered Delilah
    a) 1100 pieces of silver each.
    b) a nose ring.
    c) a pet lizard.
    d) two large ruby rings for her toes.

2. What king of Gath fell for David's trick of feigning insanity—and let him go free?

3. Connect the Thoughts:
    Othniel
    Jair
    Elon

4. In what part of their houses were the ancient Israelites to write God's commands, as a daily reminder to themselves and their children?

5. Match: Obadiah. . .
    a) led Jezebel to find Elijah.
    b) refused Elisha's demand that he tell Ahab he had found the prophet.
    c) was in charge of Ahab's palace.

ANSWERS

1. a (Judges 16:5)
2. Achish (1 Samuel 21:10–15)
3. judges of Israel (Judges 3:9–10; Judges 10:3; Judges 12:11)
4. doorposts (Deuteronomy 11:18–20)
5. c (1 Kings 18:3)

Day 355

1. True or False: David's brothers were sure David could easily slay Goliath.

2. Because of what miracle did the Sanhedrin plot to take Jesus' life?

3. Connect the Thoughts:
   wars and rumours of wars
   famines, pestilences, and earthquakes
   false prophets

4. Immediately after Peter had denied Jesus three times, a
   a) donkey brayed.
   b) fire engine siren went off.
   c) rooster crowed.
   d) woman screamed.

5. What was the requirement for male slaves and foreigners to eat the Passover meal?

ANSWERS

1. False (1 Samuel 17:28)
2. raising Lazarus from the dead (John 11:44–53)
3. signs of Christ's coming (Matthew 24:3–14 KJV)
4. c (John 18:15–18, 25–27)
5. circumcision (Exodus 12:43–49)

Day 356

1. What does Romans 1 say reveals the invisible attributes of God?

2. Once you stop living for sin, you are guided by
   a) your minister.
   b) your Sunday school teacher.
   c) your friends.
   d) the Holy Spirit.

3. What two things will you find if you live in the Spirit?

4. God promised the Israelites
   a) forty acres and a mule.
   b) a land flowing with milk and honey.
   c) straw for bricks.
   d) great riches.

5. What does Psalm 103:17–18 say is everlasting to those who keep God's covenants?

ANSWERS

1. the creation of the world (Romans 1:20)
2. d (Romans 8:1)
3. life and peace (Romans 8:6)
4. b (Exodus 3:8)
5. His mercy

Day 357

1. Which disciple, according to Luke, ran to Jesus' tomb after faithful women told him of the Lord's resurrection?

2. When Jesus called Matthew to follow him, Matthew was
   a) sitting at the receipt of custom, or tax collector's booth.
   b) praying.
   c) making a traditional wave offering.
   d) persecuting Christians.

3. Connect the Thoughts:
   the death of Judas Iscariot
   eleven apostles
   the drawing of lots

4. Match: Titus. . .
   a) was supposed to meet Paul in Troas.
   b) was left by Paul on the island of Malta.
   c) was raised from the dead at Troas.

5. Which two apostles raised people from the dead?

ANSWERS

1. Peter (Luke 24:1–12)
2. a (Matthew 9:9)
3. Matthias (Acts 1:18–26)
4. a (2 Corinthians 2:12–13)
5. Peter (Acts 9:36–43) and Paul (Acts 20:9–10)

Day 358

1. Where did Solomon obtain the cedar with which he built the Lord's Temple?
   a) Lebanon
   b) Sinai
   c) Egypt
   d) Cyprus

2. What Philistine city's name is still heard in the news today, often with the word "strip"?

3. Connect the Thoughts:
   Seleucia
   Cyprus
   Salamis

4. Match: Jabbok. . .
   a) what Joshua crossed to enter Canaan
   b) near where Jacob wrestled with God
   c) called the border of the Canaanites

5. What country did Joseph, Mary, and the baby Jesus flee to for safety from King Herod's murderous anger?

ANSWERS

1. a (1 Kings 5:5–9)
2. Gaza (2 Kings 18:8)
3. stops on Paul's missionary journeys (Acts 13:2–5)
4. b (Genesis 32:22–30)
5. Egypt (Matthew 2:13)

Day 359

1. Connect the Thoughts:
    Bartimaeus
    Peter's mother-in-law
    Jairus' daughter

2. When Jesus chose Matthew, Jesus had just
    a) forgiven the sins of a sick man.
    b) enabled a man with palsy to walk.
    c) showed scribes His authority to forgive sin.
    d) all of the above.

3. Where is Jesus now?

4. When Jesus comes a second time, where will He appear, and on what?

5. What will we do if we love Jesus?

ANSWERS

1. people healed by Jesus (Mark 10:46–52; Luke 4:38–39; Mark 5:21–43)
2. d (Matthew 9:1–9)
3. He sits at the right hand of the throne of God (Hebrews 12:2).
4. in the sky on clouds (Matthew 24:30)
5. We will keep his commandments (John 14:15).

Day 360

1. Which of the following precious stones is not part of the new Jerusalem's foundation?
   a) diamond
   b) sapphire
   c) emerald
   d) amethyst

2. What jewel did Jesus warn against throwing to pigs?

3. Connect the Thoughts:
   King David's palace
   the behemoth's tail
   Lebanon

4. What bunched herb was to be dipped in blood during the first Passover?

5. According to the book of Revelation, the streets of the new Jerusalem are made of what?
   a) gold
   b) silver
   c) cedar
   d) asphalt

ANSWERS

1. a (Revelation 21:19–20)
2. pearls (Matthew 7:6)
3. cedar (2 Samuel 7:1–5; Job 40:15–17; Psalm 92:12)
4. hyssop (Exodus 12:22–27)
5. a (Revelation 21:2, 21)

Day 361

1. Connect the Thoughts:
    divisions
    lawsuits
    a man has his father's wife

2. What character in the book of Esther was hanged on a gallows that he had ordered built?
    a) Mordecai
    b) Xerxes
    c) Haman
    d) Harbona

3. Jude told his readers to remember two cities that were punished by God. What are the names of the cities?

4. Who gave King Ahab the message from God that Ahab would pay for his sin?

5. What two groups of people, according to the crowd at Jesus' crucifixion, should bear responsibility for Jesus' death?

ANSWERS

1. problems in the church at Corinth (1 Corinthians 1:10–12; 1 Corinthians 6:1–6; 1 Corinthians 5:1)
2. c (Esther 7:8–9)
3. Sodom and Gomorrah (Jude 7)
4. Elijah (1 Kings 21:17–19)
5. "us and. . .our children" (Matthew 27:25)

Day 362

1. What did the apostle Paul say should be "seasoned with salt"?

2. According to the apostle Paul, what never fails?
   a) love
   b) truth
   c) faith
   d) God

3. Whom did Jesus say watches over children?

4. According to the apostle Paul, how are husbands supposed to love their wives?
   a) as Abraham cared for Sarah
   b) as Christ loved the church
   c) as the Spirit gives them power
   d) as the hen protects her chicks

5. According to the Ten Commandments, what will happen if we honor our father and mother?

ANSWERS

1. conversation, or speech (Colossians 4:6)
2. a (1 Corinthians 13:8 NIV)
3. their angels in heaven (Matthew 18:10)
4. b (Ephesians 5:25)
5. your days will be long (Exodus 20:12)

Day 363

1. What mournful clothing did the people of Nineveh wear to show their repentance before God?

2. Connect the Thoughts:
   Jair's sons
   Jesus' age of ministry
   Judas' pieces of silver

3. Complete the scripture:
   I reckon that the sufferings of this present time are not worthy to be compared with the ___ which shall be revealed in us.

4. What is the last word in the book of Matthew?

5. What are the names of the twelve tribes of Israel?

ANSWERS

1. sackcloth (Jonah 3:5)
2. thirty (Judges 10:3–4; Luke 3:23; Matthew 27:3)
3. glory (Romans 8:18 KJV)
4. Amen
5. Dan, Asher, Naphtali, Judah, Issachar, Zebulun, Reuben, Simeon, Gad, Ephraim, Manasseh, and Benjamin

Day 364

1. What is the one requirement Jesus gives for receiving eternal life (salvation)?

2. How does John 3:16 begin?

3. Which of the disciples said to Jesus, "Thou hast the words of eternal life"?
   a) John
   b) Peter
   c) James
   d) Andrew

4. What word, according to Jesus, describes the way or road that "leadeth unto life"?

5. What did John, in his first letter, want "you that believe on the name of the Son of God" to "know that ye have"?
   a) peace and joy
   b) eternal life
   c) comfort from the Spirit
   d) wisdom and truth

ANSWERS

1. to believe in Him (John 3:16)
2. "For God so loved the world. . . ." (John 3:16)
3. b (John 6:68–69 KJV)
4. narrow (Matthew 7:13–14)
5. b (1 John 5:13 KJV)

Day 365

1. What future Israelite leader, as a baby, was described as "no ordinary child" or "exceeding fair" ?

2. Match: Widow at Zarephath. . .
   a) Elisha told her she would have food until the rains came.
   b) Elisha asked her for a piece of bread.
   c) Elijah prayed for her son's life.

3. Connect the Thoughts
   twelve tribes
   also known as Jacob
   God's chosen people

4. At first, Samson told Delilah that he would be weak if he were
   a) shaven.
   b) made to fast for three days.
   c) tied with seven green cords of rope.
   d) forced to drink nothing but fruit juice for three weeks.

5. What did Ruth offer to do if Naomi would let her stay with her?
   a) give her a new car every year until her death
   b) keep house for her
   c) find Naomi a new husband
   d) convert to Judaism

ANSWERS

1. Moses (Acts 7:20 KJV)
2. c (1 Kings 17:7–21)
3. Israel (Genesis 49:28; Genesis 32:28; Psalm 135:4)
4. c (Judges 16:7)
5. d (Ruth 1:16)

Notes

Notes

Notes

Notes

Notes

Notes

Notes

Notes

Notes

Notes

Notes

Notes